The Open University

Arts: A Fourth Level Course
Units 14–15

Thought and Reality: Central Themes in Wittgenstein's
Philosophy

LANGUAGE AND REALITY: PHILOSOPHICAL INVESTIGATIONS 1–137

Prepared by Stuart Brown
for the Course Team

The Open University Press

The cover shows a Mesolithic rock painting (6,000 B.C.) from a cave at Valltorta, Spain.
Based on a photograph by Ronald Sheridan.

The Open University Press
Walton Hall, Milton Keynes
MK7 6AA

First published 1976

Designed by the Media Development Group of the Open University.

Produced in Great Britain by
Technical Filmsetters Europe Limited, 76 Great Bridgewater Street, Manchester M1 5JY.

ISBN 0 335 05205 3

This text forms part of an Open University course. The complete list of units in the course appears at the end of this text.

For general availability of supporting material referred to in this text, please write to the Director of Marketing, The Open University, P.O. Box 81, Walton Hall, Milton Keynes, MK7 6AT.

Further information on Open University courses may be obtained from the Admissions Office, The Open University, P.O. Box 48, Walton Hall, Milton Keynes, MK7 6AB.

1.1

Arts: A Fourth Level Course
Thought and Reality: Central Themes in Wittgenstein's Philosophy

Units 14-15

Language and Reality

Philosophical Investigations 1–137

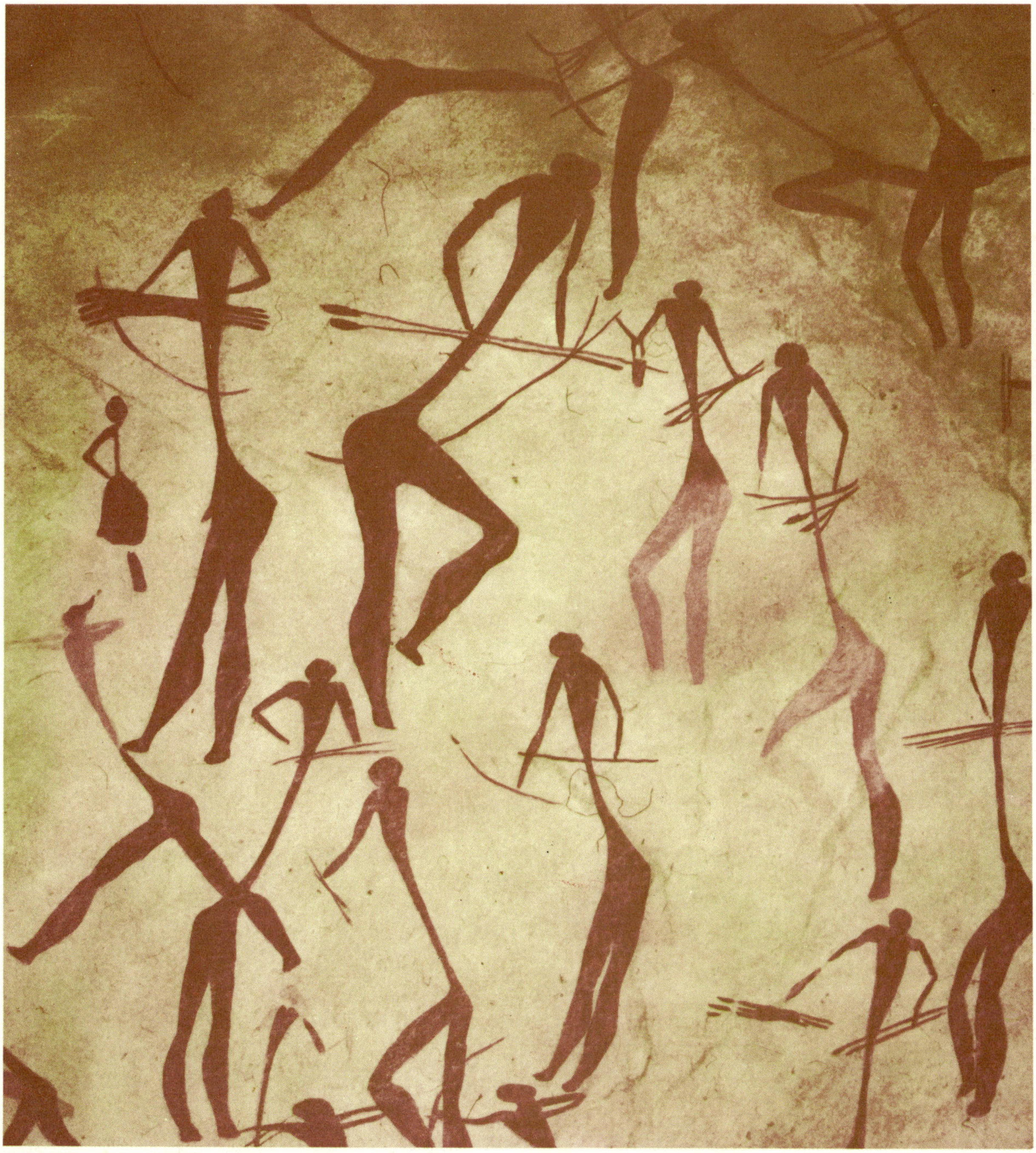

CONTENTS

1   INTRODUCTION   5

2   NAMES, SIMPLES AND OSTENSIVE DEFINITION
          (*PI* 1–64)   9
2.1   A 'picture' of the essence of language (*PI* 1–7)   9
2.1.1   Philosophical 'pictures'   12
2.2   The diversity of language (*PI* 8–25)   13
2.3   Naming and ostensive definition (*PI* 26–37)   17
2.3.1   The *Tractatus* and ostensive definition   20
2.4   Names and simples (*PI* 38–47)   22
2.5   The metaphysics of logical atomism (*PI* 48–59)   28
2.6   Wittgenstein's rejection of analysis (*PI* 60–64)   30

3   LOGIC AND THE ESSENCE OF LANGUAGE (*PI* 65–137)   34
3.1   An alternative to essentialism (*PI* 65–91)   36
3.1.1   Games and 'family resemblances' (*PI* 66–69)   37
3.1.2   The demand for definiteness of sense (*PI* 70–91)   39
3.1.3   The theory of descriptions (*PI* 79f.)   43
3.2   Logic and 'the a priori order of the world' (*PI* 92–108)   45
3.2.1   The 'harmony between thought and reality' (*PI* 93–97)   48
3.3   The 'business of philosophy' (*PI* 109–133)   51
3.4   Towards a 'clear view' of our use of 'proposition' (*PI* 134–137)   55

QUESTIONS FOR DISCUSSION AND REVISION   62

FURTHER READING   63

ABBREVIATIONS

The following abbreviations will be used in these units to refer to prescribed texts. These are all texts you should have to hand in working through this material, as well as Units 5–10.

Wittgenstein

T   *Tractatus Logico-Philosophicus*, 1921, trans. D. F. Pears and B. F. McGuinness, Routledge and Kegan Paul, 1961. Followed by Wittgenstein's proposition number, common to all editions.

BB   *The Blue and Brown Books*, with preface by R. Rhees, Oxford, Basil Blackwell, 1958. Followed by page number, common to paperback edition.

PI   *Philosophical Investigations*, ed. G. E. M. Anscombe and R. Rhees, trans. G. E. M. Anscombe, Oxford, Basil Blackwell, 1953. The number following the abbreviation refers to the passage of Part I so numbered by Wittgenstein. References to Part II will give the section and, in some cases, the page number, prefaced by 'p.', common to paperback edition.

Russell

References to Russell's 1917–18 lectures on 'The Philosophy of Logical Atomism' will be, as in earlier units, to two editions:

1   *Russell's Logical Atomism*, ed. D. F. Pears, Fontana, 1972, referred to as '*RLA*', followed by a page number.

2   *Logic and Knowledge*, ed. R. C. Marsh, Allen and Unwin, 1956, referred to as '*LK*', followed by a page number.

1   INTRODUCTION

These units are the first of a large block in which you will have a chance to study the later thought of Wittgenstein in some detail. Up to this point the course has covered a considerable range of divergent approaches to a number of basic philosophical problems, about meaning, truth, the relation of language to experience and to the world, and so on. You have also had an opportunity to consider Wittgenstein's earlier views on some of these subjects in his *Tractatus Logico-Philosophicus* and have already glimpsed some of the changes which were taking place in his so-called 'transitional' period (1929–33). The course has not emphasized this period of transition from the ideas of the *Tractatus* to those of the *Investigations*. Hence neither of the large works written by Wittgenstein during this period—the *Philosophische Bemerkungen* (1930) and the *Philosophische Grammatik* (1932)[1]—is a prescribed text.

Wittgenstein's later philosophy has had a profound influence on the development of British philosophy since the Second World War. Some of the ideas he put forward seemed so new that he came to be regarded as a quite different philosopher from the author of the *Tractatus*. G. H. von Wright, in a biographical sketch, wrote:[2]

> ... Wittgenstein's new philosophy is, so far as I can see, entirely outside any philosophical tradition and without literary sources of influence. For this reason it is extremely difficult to understand and to characterize. The author of the *Tractatus* had learned from Frege and Russell. His problems grew out of theirs. The author of the *Investigations* has no ancestors in philosophy.

The implication of von Wright's remarks is that Wittgenstein's later philosophy constitutes a complete break with that of the *Tractatus*. This view was rather encouraged by Wittgenstein himself. In his Preface to the *Philosophical Investigations*, Wittgenstein wrote of the 'grave errors' of the *Tractatus*. True, he insisted that his new thoughts 'could be seen in the right light only by contrast with and against the background of my old way of thinking'. But many of these 'new thoughts' are expressed in opposition to the *Tractatus* and from a standpoint of some intellectual distance. The topics are, of course, often the same—concepts such as 'meaning' and 'proposition' and problems about the nature of logic are to the fore—but the manner in which they are treated is altogether different from anything you might be led to expect from reading the *Tractatus*.

There are difficulties for students arising from the novel style of writing adopted by Wittgenstein in his later writings. To begin with, Wittgenstein does not always speak 'in his own voice'. Often his remarks take the form of a discussion with an imaginary interlocutor. This other point of view is frequently indicated by the use of inverted commas. (e.g. *PI* 100) But Wittgenstein does not adhere to a strict convention. A remarkable feature of his later writing is the number of sentences which end with a question mark. Often, indeed, he gives no answer to the question he raises. In these cases we can, I think, reasonably assume that he is not attributing the question to an

---

[1] These works are now available in English translation, respectively as *Philosophical Grammar*, trans. Anthony Kenny, Blackwell, 1974 and *Philosophical Remarks*, trans. Raymond Hargreaves and Roger White, Blackwell, 1975. Both works are edited by Rush Rhees.

[2] In *Ludwig Wittgenstein: A Memoir*, by Norman Malcolm, Oxford, 1958, Oxford Paperbacks, 1962, p. 15.

imaginary interlocutor. Sometimes he is raising a question to which he implies no answer, but which he raises to provoke his reader. At other times the question is a rhetorical one.

Wittgenstein's change of style, from the tightly structured formal presentation of the *Tractatus* to a way of writing which is often conversational, is indicative of a change in his conception of philosophy. This becomes apparent if we consider questions about the role and identity of this 'imaginary interlocutor'. It might be thought that this is merely a device which Wittgenstein makes use of, that the 'second voice' introduced in the discussions is merely a straw man whose role is that of spokesman for any of a variety of wrong-headed opinions. I think that this is a fundamentally mistaken view. I suggest that you consider, when you come across passages with such an element of dialogue, the possibility that this 'second voice' is Wittgenstein's own, or at least the voice of someone with whom Wittgenstein is to some extent *tempted* to agree. Of course Wittgenstein does not often agree with this 'second voice'. On the contrary its suggestions are often rejected with vehemence. The tone, however, is not that of someone who is contemptuously dismissing criticism coming from the standpoint of an outmoded style of thinking. Certain ways of philosophical thinking seemed to Wittgenstein to represent something of a *disease* of the human mind. Philosophy, he insisted, is a 'struggle against the bewitchment of our intelligence by means of language'. (*PI* 109) This, for Wittgenstein, is an *internal* struggle, an attempt to cure oneself of something analogous to a mental illness. Wittgenstein was no 'enlightenment' thinker after the manner of the Vienna Circle, with some set of formulas to cure the ills of philosophy. Those ills he saw as running deep. Only 'complete clarity' would bring them to an end. (*PI* 133) I do not think that Wittgenstein supposed for one moment that he had attained to such clarity. There is a saying of Luther that in the midst of life we are surrounded by death. Wittgenstein once suggested that it might be said, in something of that spirit, that in the midst of sanity we are surrounded by madness. The illnesses of philosophy, he thought, had to be allowed to run their course. And this means that the 'second voice' must be allowed to express itself and indeed be taken seriously. Wittgenstein's strategy demands that the 'second voice' be treated, not as that of a heckler or a fool, but as someone who, in a sense, speaks for *us*. If we cannot immediately sympathize with what the 'interlocutor' says, it is worth trying to understand the position from which he speaks. Otherwise we are likely to find difficulty in seeing the force of Wittgenstein's reply.

Another difficulty in the style of the *Investigations* arises from the appearance it can give of being a collection of remarks of a fragmentary and self-contained kind. In his Preface, indeed, Wittgenstein appears to concede that 'this book is really only an album'. (*PI* p. *ix*) Now it is true that Wittgenstein did cut up his typescripts into separate fragments. A collection of such fragments—*Zettel*—has indeed been published. But he also attached a great deal of importance to putting these fragments in a satisfactory order. In the process of improving on earlier manuscripts he would add new sections, delete others and alter the arrangement of the sections. In his Preface, Wittgenstein writes that he had not succeeded in welding his 'results' into a satisfactory whole. His remark that the *Investigations* is 'really only an album' is an expression of dissatisfaction and, so far from confirming the view that it is merely a collection of fragments, is actually evidence against it. Because of its more finished character, the arrangement of the *Investigations*—the placing of the sections in relation to one another—cannot be assumed to be haphazard. On the contrary the point of what is being said, as we shall see, often turns on the context in which a given section is placed.

The arrangement of the *Investigations* is quite different from that of the *Tractatus*. In the 'dogmatic'—as he later called it—mode of the *Tractatus*, the decimal numbering of sections was designed to bring out which sections were subordinate to which. The sections of the *Investigations* are on a much more equal footing. Wittgenstein no longer thought of what he was doing as advancing theses, which would then need amplification and defence. (*PI* 128) Philosophy, as he now saw it, only provides a rearrangement of what everyone knows already. 'Philosophy simply puts everything before us, and neither explains nor deduces anything.' (*PI* 126) The 'problems' of philosophy are not solved by giving 'new information' but rather 'by arranging what we have always known'. (*PI* 109)

This does not, of course, mean that philosophy is easy. For all the time the results that have so far been obtained may be put in question. It even seems that no philosophical problems have been solved until all philosophical problems have been solved, as if nothing less than '*complete* clarity' will do. (*PI* 133) The *Blue Book* gives a 'rough answer' to this statement:

> It is, that every new problem which arises may put in question the *position* which our previous partial results are to occupy in the final picture. One then speaks of having to reinterpret these previous results; and we should say: they have to be placed in a different surrounding.

> Imagine we had to arrange the books of a library. When we begin the books lie higgledy-piggledy on the floor. Now there would be many ways of sorting them and putting them in their places. One would be to take the books one by one and put each on the shelf in its right place. On the other hand we might take up several books from the floor and put them in a row on a shelf, merely in order to indicate that these books ought to go together in this order. In the course of arranging the library this whole row of books will have to change its place. But it would be wrong to say that therefore putting them together on a shelf was no step towards the final result. In this case, in fact, it is pretty obvious that having put together books which belong together was a definite achievement, even though the whole row of them had to be shifted. But some of the greatest achievements in philosophy could only be compared with taking up some books which seemed to belong together, and putting them on different shelves; nothing more being final about their positions than that they no longer lie side by side. (*BB* 44f.)

In the *Investigations* the metaphor has changed. Wittgenstein's 'results' are now represented as sketches of landscapes made during a complicated journey over 'a wide field of thought'. (*PI* p. *ix*) These also need to be 'arranged' so that 'if you looked at them you could get a picture of the landscape', something like a bird's-eye-view. The consequence of a good arrangement is that things that had seemed far apart—had, in the earlier metaphor, been placed on different shelves—are now seen as closer together, as perhaps happens with language and games in the early sections of the *Investigations*. Equally such an arrangement will show that certain things we are inclined to group together should be kept quite apart. An example of this is the belief that a word acquires meaning by being attached, like a label, to something and that the meaning of a word is what it is the name of. These are good examples of the kinds of rearrangement which cannot be undertaken without further implications. If we separate a word's meaning from what it stands for, we need to put in place the role of pointing to something as part of an explanation of what one means, and so on. This is closely connected with the need to take the 'second voice' seriously, with the idea forcibly expressed in Wittgenstein's remark: 'Philosophical mistakes contain so much truth.' (*Zettel* 460) To get to the source of philosophical error we need to see what is right about it. In the *Blue Book* Wittgenstein wrote: 'The man who is philosophically puzzled sees a law in the way a word is used, and, trying to apply this law consistently, comes up against cases where it leads to paradoxical results.' (*BB* 27) Such a man does not have a clear view of how the word in question is used. On the other hand his 'seeing' *that* law in the way the word is used may reflect some aspect of its use. The roots of the problems which arise through 'misinterpretation of our forms of language' are, Wittgenstein wrote, 'as deep in us as the forms of our language'. (*PI* 111) The kind of clarity which a good arrangement would bring would make these problems disappear. (*PI* 133) It is in relation to this ideal, perhaps, that Wittgenstein felt the *Investigations* to be a failure.

However that may be, the part of the *Investigations* we shall be studying in these units seems to me to come as close as any part of Wittgenstein's writing to the kind of arrangement he sought. The discussions do seem to 'proceed from one subject to another in a natural order' so that the discussion of one topic throws light on the discussion of the next, each contributing to an overall 'picture of the landscape'. The problems of the *Tractatus* give a special point and unity to these sections. For this reason too they provide a good starting-point for the study of Wittgenstein's later philosophy. For if that later philosophy can be given an intelligible exposition without reference to the *Tractatus*, the same cannot be said of Wittgenstein's own exposition of it.

Broadcasting

The broadcasting component of these units consists of a radio talk (Radio Programme 09) by Anthony Quinton on some of the salient points of departure in Wittgenstein's later philosophy.

Acknowledgments

My colleagues, Oswald Hanfling and Carolyn Wilde, and Professor Peter Winch of King's College, London, have commented very helpfully on drafts of this material. I would like to record my gratitude to them.

2 NAMES, SIMPLES AND OSTENSIVE DEFINITION (*PI* 1–64)

One of the aims of these units is that of introducing you to reading the *Investigations*. That is partly why the scope of our discussions will extend to nearly a quarter of that book. It also happens that *PI* 1–137 brings in some of the main ideas of the later philosophy through criticism of the doctrines and approach of the *Tractatus*. It will not be possible for us to examine all of these passages with the same degree of attention. But some of the passages I shall gloss over are ones which, from your earlier work on the course and your study of this material, you should be in a position to work through on your own. Since, however, I want to bring out the importance of Wittgenstein's *arrangement* of his material, I shall indicate how I think the discussions we do not examine in detail relate to the discussions to which we are going to give particular attention.

It has seemed to me right to divide up the material so that we can discuss it in manageable sections. In doing so, however, I am imposing a different division of Wittgenstein's material from that of the *Investigations* itself. There are clear gains in ease of exposition from doing this. But it is important not to compartmentalize your thinking about Wittgenstein under the headings of my sections. It is not that my sections are arbitrary. But the discussions should not be isolated from one another. Thus, while *PI* 1–137 can indeed be divided into two main sections—as my arrangement of this material suggests—*PI* 65 makes it clear that 'the great question that lies behind all these considerations' which he had adduced up to that point is about the essence of language. That question unites the discussion of names, simples and ostensive definition (which dominates 1–64) with the ensuing discussion in which a prominent theme is criticism of the *Tractatus*' idea of a general form of propositions. Similar considerations apply to my lesser divisions of the material as well as to my dividing off *PI* 1–137 from the later sections. Thus *PI* 138 leads off by putting an objection to what has just been claimed in *PI* 137.

With this *caveat*, let us begin by looking at the opening sections of the *Investigations*. (*PI* 1–7) When you have read them, please consider, and make a note of your answers to, the following questions:

(a) What conception of the essence of human language is Wittgenstein concerned to criticize?

(b) What affinities does this conception have with the view of language put forward in the *Tractatus*? (Give references to the *Tractatus* if you can.)

(c) What is a 'language-game'? What is the relation between a 'language-game' and what is referred to in *PI* 2 as a 'complete primitive language'?

(d) What role does the idea of a 'language-game' play in Wittgenstein's criticism of Augustine's conception of language?

2.1 A 'PICTURE' OF THE ESSENCE OF LANGUAGE (*PI* 1–7)

(a) The conception Wittgenstein is concerned to criticize is that the individual words of language are the names of objects and that sentences are combinations of such names. This is the view Wittgenstein attributes to Augustine in *PI* 1. It is a conception of the *essence* of language insofar as it treats any other use of words as secondary or peripheral, 'as something that

Language games — use not meaning object.

— form of life.

will take care of itself'. The main job of explaining how words have meaning, and how that meaning is learnt, is done once it is shown how words are correlated with objects and thus come to mean them.

(b)   Although Augustine's account is by no means as rarefied as that of the *Tractatus*, Wittgenstein's account of the picture Augustine's words give us of the essence of language is strikingly reminiscent of the *Tractatus*: e.g.

> It is obvious that the analysis of propositions must bring us to elementary propositions which consist of names in immediate combination. (*T* 4.221)

> A name means an object. The object is its meaning. (*T* 3.203)

(c)   The idea of a language-*game* is evidently inspired by 'those games by means of which children learn their native language'. (*PI* 7) They are games in which words and actions go together, in which words are learnt by doing certain things: e.g. the meaning of 'all fall down' is learnt in the context of these words being said as everyone collapses on the floor, 'ring' is learnt by forming a ring, and so on. (Ring-a-ring-a-roses is Wittgenstein's example in *PI* 7, para. 3.) One of the features of language which Wittgenstein wishes to bring into prominence in talking about language-*games* is the fact that the *speaking* of language is, as he later puts it, 'part of an activity, or of a form of life'. Here, in *PI* 7, para. 4, he *defines* a 'language-game' as 'the whole, consisting of language and the actions into which it is woven'. He is not making the point that, as it happens, we *usually* make use of language in the context of doing something. That would be a trivial point which no one would be tempted to deny. His point is, rather, that language cannot be separated from human activities. The two are inter-woven. You cannot imagine language on its own since 'to imagine a language means to imagine a form of life'. (*PI* 19)

Children's language-games are, of course, much simpler than those of adults. In that sense they are more 'primitive'. Learning more complicated language-games—the implication of *PI* 5 seems to be—may involve *explanation*. Perhaps teaching a child about money—about buying and selling—would involve the child in such a more complicated language-game, which needed explanation. But then it already assumes the child has mastered more elementary language-games, e.g. of wanting and giving. At the level of 'primitive forms of language' no explanation is involved, since presumably there is no verbal currency in which to offer one, but only *training*. The child is just trained to act in certain ways. It is not *explained* to him what 'red' is, what 'five' means, and so on. He is simply *trained* in the use of these words. 'Explanations', Wittgenstein says (*PI* 1), 'come to an end somewhere.'

You may have been puzzled at Wittgenstein's remark that the question as to what the word 'five' *means* is not relevant here. You may also have been puzzled as to who is asking the question 'But what is the meaning of the word "five"?' This is the first of many points in the *Investigations* where Wittgenstein's writing takes on the form of a dialogue. This is the 'second voice' to which I referred in the Introduction. Here it speaks in a spirit of objection, in the tone of voice of one who is not satisfied with the remark, 'Explanations come to an end somewhere'. It is the same person who has asked, 'But how does he know ... what he is to do with the word "five"?' The implication is that this *must* have been *explained* to him, that he must have learnt the meaning of the word 'five', or else he would not be able to do what is asked of him. But this leads us to ask the wrong question: 'What is the meaning of the word "five"?' That question, Wittgenstein rejoins, is

To follow a rule.

? not relevant here, but only how the word 'five' is used. The force of this remark is not wholly clear, taken in isolation from the discussions that are to follow. It is connected with the point made in *PI* 5, that children are *trained* to use words, that words are not, in the first place, *explained* to them. There is nothing more to a child's knowing the meaning of the word 'five' than his being able to use it, i.e. acting in the right way when asked to fetch 'five red apples', and so on. The 'second voice' here is the voice of someone who feels there *must* be something more.

The temptation to insist that there must be something more to knowing what the word 'five' means, than *just* being able to use it, has many roots. But one root, as the context indicates, is the 'picture' of the essence of language attributed to Augustine. That 'picture' encourages the idea that the meaning of a word is something for which the object stands. There would, on that account, be something which could be called 'knowing the meaning of a word' and which, so far from *consisting* in being able to use it correctly, was what *accounted for* being able to use it correctly. From that standpoint it would appear that Wittgenstein was giving a superficial account, that something more had to be said to explain how someone could say 'five red apples' and mean something by those words or, as in this case, hear those words and understand something by them.

Of course there is more to be *said*. But what more needs to be said is not by way of the explanation sought but by way of clarification of what it is to take part in a language-game. An important dimension of this is introduced by Wittgenstein's discussions of what it is to follow a rule. These belong outside of the scope of these units and are taken up in Units 16–19, Sect. 2.

Let us return, then, to the question we are specifically concerned with at this point. A 'complete primitive language' is a simple language-game which we can consider on its own, one we could imagine as 'the whole language of a tribe'. (*PI* 6) If we can imagine this, as Wittgenstein implies we can, we should be supposing that there is a language within which there is no room for explanation of how language is to be used. The language, we might say, does not contain the materials for such explanations and functions without them. 'The children are brought up to perform *these* actions, to use *these* words as they do so, and to react in *this* way to the words of others.' (*PI* 6, para. 1)' Language would not be explained to those children. They would simply be trained in its use. Not all language is like this. (Though it is a point of some importance in Wittgenstein's later philosophy that all language is founded in the last resort on training rather than explanation or justification.) Thus a 'primitive language' is just one kind of language-game.

(d)   Wittgenstein's strategy is designed to bring out what truth there is in this view of language by imagining a simple language for which the account being criticized is right. This is the 'language-game' of *PI* 2. We could imagine that this was the *whole* language of the builder A and his assistant B, even that it was 'the whole language of a tribe'. (*PI* 6) That this is an over-simple conception of language is brought out by contrasting the language of *PI* 2, for which it *does* work, with the example in *PI* 1, for which it does not. If we suppose that every word which has a meaning stands for some object, we are led into the difficulties Wittgenstein mentions in *PI* 5. An 'inkling' of those difficulties is given, he says, in the example in *PI* 1. They arise because that supposition leads us to ask the wrong questions. It leads us to ask 'What is the meaning of the word "five"?' Wittgenstein rejects that question—'No such thing was in question here, only how the word "five" is used.' The fact that such a question is asked is a sign of confusion. In Wittgenstein's metaphor 'this general notion of the meaning of a word surrounds the

11

working of language with a haze which makes clear vision impossible'. (*PI* 5) By imagining primitive languages we can extract ourselves from such confusion. For in these cases we can command a clear view of the aim and functioning of the words. We can imagine a language-game in which the words do function in the way in which, on Augustine's account, words always do. But when we do this it comes out that this is a very restricted view of language, one with limited applicability. Augustine is likened to the man who says 'A game consists in...' and then goes on to describe what is only *one kind* of game.

2.1.1 Philosophical 'pictures'

In *PI* 1 Wittgenstein says of Augustine's words that they give us a particular 'picture' of the essence of human language. As I expect you will have gathered from the way 'picture' is used in the *Tractatus*, it is a translation of a German word ('Bild') whose connotations are rather broader than the word 'picture' in ordinary English. It may be a sufficient explanation of this use of 'picture' if we noted that the word 'Bild' might, in this context, equally be translated 'model'. But I am inclined to think that it is no coincidence that Wittgenstein uses the same word here as he did in the *Tractatus* in saying that the proposition is 'a picture of reality'. (4.01) As we shall see, (Section 3.2.1), Wittgenstein came to reject the view that the difference between proposition and reality was somehow ironed out by the pictorial character of the proposition itself. He had assumed that 'no further room is left for a method of application, but only for agreement and disagreement'. (*Philosophical Grammar*, p. 214) With a picture it *seems* as if you get straight through to reality and can be quite certain that things are as depicted. It seems as if it is a question of seeing an intrinsic connection between the way the elements of the picture are arranged and the way in which the corresponding elements in the world are arranged. Just as Dürer, looking at the object he wanted to draw through a transparent screen on which he had traced the outlines of the object, might be said to have simply seen the harmony between his picture and the reality it portrayed, so in essence do we compare our propositions with the world.

Wittgenstein came to regard this view as an 'illusion'. (*PI* 96) But it was not an illusion like an ordinary mistake, such as supposing that a (straight) stick which looks bent when seen in water really is bent. In an ordinary illusion, any temptation to error can be removed by drawing attention to the facts, e.g. by pulling the stick out of the water to show that it is really straight and then putting it back again. But the kinds of illusion to which philosophers are prone are much more seductive. They acquire a power over our minds which it is difficult to shake off. They do this because of their association with the feeling we have that things *must* be as we take them to be, that we have somehow penetrated to the essence of the matter, e.g. to the essence of what a proposition is, of what language is. Once that idea is established in our minds it cannot be removed simply by pointing to apparent exceptions. For the existence of apparent exceptions is already conceded in advance by someone who is offering an account of the *essence* of language. (See, e.g., *T* 4.002.) Indeed, in his account of language-games in *The Blue Book*, in which Wittgenstein stresses the advantage of examining primitive forms of language if we want to study such problems as those of 'truth and falsehood, of the agreement and disagreement of propositions with reality, of the nature of assertion, assumption, and question', he recognizes the obstacle to such an examination. '... what makes it difficult for us to take this line of investigation is our craving for generality'. (*BB* 17) One source of that

Something in common
– essence

'craving' is the belief that there must be something common to all the entities we subsume under a general term. In Section 3 we shall be looking at the view that there must be something common to what we call 'propositions', in regard to which Wittgenstein discusses whether there is something common to what we call 'games'. (*PI* 66–75) That view, that propositions must all have something in common, is an immediate consequence of the belief that there is an *essence* of propositions. Indeed Wittgenstein seems to have regarded the question about the *'essence'* of a language-game as identical with the question 'What is *common* to these activities in virtue of which they constitute language or parts of language?' (Cf. *PI* 65)

You will find the word 'picture' frequently used in Wittgenstein's later writings of ideas which tend to become fixed in people's minds but which they find it difficult to apply. (See, e.g., *PI* 352, *PI* 373f., *PI* 422ff., *BB* 56.) The 'picture theory' of the *Tractatus* is itself such a picture. In *PI* 115, with reference to the *Tractatus* account of the essence of propositions, Wittgenstein writes: 'A *picture* held us captive. And we could not get outside it, for it lay in our language and language seemed to repeat it to us inexorably.' It is this consideration—that a picture we may have of the essence of something, or of how things 'must' be, involves our looking at things in such a way that our fixed idea is constantly re-enforced—which stands in the way of 'an examination of details in philosophy'. (*PI* 52) Yet the discrepancy between those details about the use people actually do or might make of language and the philosopher's pictures of what language is really like shows the difficulty of applying those pictures. The sense of a philosophical *problem* arises because of an awareness of this discrepancy. It is not, however, that philosophers are just unaware of the workings of language. Rather they have an *urge* to misunderstand them. (*PI* 109) In the *Tractatus* Wittgenstein had expressed the view that most of the questions and propositions of philosophers arise from 'a failure to understand the logic of our language'. (*T* 4.003) In the *Investigations* that sentiment seems echoed by such phrases as 'misunderstanding of the logic of language'. (*PI* 93) But there is at least this important difference. In the *Tractatus* the misunderstandings were to be cleared up by pointing out errors which logical analysis exposes. (See Units 7–10, Sect. VII.3.) But philosophical 'pictures', such as that Augustine's words are said to give us of the essence of language, are not to be dispelled in this way. The process of breaking the hold they have is both more complex and more roundabout. That is partly why Wittgenstein's reasoning in the *Investigations* is very different in character from that of the earlier work.

intention

2.2   THE DIVERSITY OF LANGUAGE (*PI* 8–25)

Wittgenstein began his discussion of Augustine's 'picture' of the essence of human language—namely that 'the individual words in language name objects' and 'sentences are combinations of such names'—by producing an example which appears not to fit it. In the example (*PI* 1) someone is sent shopping with the words 'five red apples' written on a slip. These words, construed as a combination of names, invite the question 'What is the meaning of the word "five"?' It is clear from the outset that Wittgenstein wants to reject a picture which makes us ask such confused questions. It is, I think, against *this* view that the slogan 'Don't ask for the meaning, ask for the use!'—which has been attributed to Wittgenstein—might most appropriately be directed. In *PI* 1 he concludes by remarking that no such thing as the meaning of the word 'five' was in question in his example, only how the word is used. Later on (in *PI* 43) he claims that for a large class of cases the meaning of a word is 'its use in the language'. A positive doctrine of meaning is already hinted at in the criticism put forward of the view that the meaning of a word is the object for which it stands. We shall return to this positive doctrine at a later stage. I mention it now because it is closely connected with the view that 'the *speaking* of language is part of an activity, or of a form of life', an idea to which Wittgenstein intended to 'bring into prominence' (*PI* 23) by his choice of the term 'language-*game*'.

The language-game in *PI* 2 is intended as an imaginary language for which the description given by Augustine is right. If you think of language in this way, you are—so Wittgenstein suggests—thinking primarily of nouns and supposing that other kinds of word will take care of themselves. Among the other kinds of word are numerals and simple predicative expressions like 'red' as well as words like 'there' and 'this' which are used in connexion with a pointing gesture. Then there are proper names. If we add words of these kinds to those in *PI* 2 we have the vocabulary of a more complicated language-game. This is what Wittgenstein does in *PI* 8 and *PI* 15, adding the first three kinds in *PI* 8 and proper names in *PI* 15. As the language-games become more complicated so we move closer to the forms of language we actually use. Augustine's picture is about the nature of *our* language. So it is not sufficient that we are able to imagine a language-game for which it is really valid. But if we start from such a language-game and then try to extend it, we can both do justice to the temptation which there is to accept such a picture of language in general and see clearly where the difficulties arise in applying it.

I suggest you now read *PI* 8–14 and make a note of your answers to the following questions:

1   Why is the question 'what do the words of this language *signify*?' raised at the beginning of *PI* 10?

2   What is Wittgenstein's response to the question?

---

1   The question as to what the words of language-game *PI* 8 *signify* is no more asked in Wittgenstein's own voice than was the question 'what is the meaning of the word "five"?' in *PI* 1. It is the same picture of the essence of language which inclines us to ask each question. Once we have said that the meaning of a word is the object for which it stands, that is the question we are unable to help asking.

2   The language-game of *PI* 8 is kept deliberately simple so that it approximates as closely as possible to the requirements of the conception of language being considered. When, in *PI* 9, the question is raised as to how a child would learn this language-game, it is allowed that it could be taught ostensively, with some reservation for 'this' and 'there'. The letters of the alphabet ('a', 'b', 'c', etc.) are imagined as numerals in this language-game. If it is thought of as restricted to the first five or six cardinal numerals the series (which we know as '1', '2', etc.) might plausibly be supposed to be taught ostensively. For then a child would learn 'd' by reference to groups of four objects whose number can be 'taken in at a glance'. A child could thus learn to fetch 'd slabs' without having learnt to count 'a', 'b', 'c', 'd' and of course without any conception of extending the series further indefinitely.

Wittgenstein thus concedes the importance of pointing in teaching words. An adult may point to groups of four things as an important part of training a child in the use of 'd'. The construction on this activity which Wittgenstein wishes to reject is that it constitutes 'explaining the meaning of "d" '. For that suggests that the *meaning* of 'd'—what 'd' *signifies*—is some kind of separate entity to which the child is introduced when it learns what 'd' means. It can be said that the child, in learning the difference between 'slab' and 'block', is being introduced to different kinds of entity. But that is because of the function of these words. The function of 'd' is different. We can say that 'd' signifies the number 4. But that does not make the use of 'd' any more like the use of 'slab'.

If we think of the meaning of a word as something it stands for we are tempted into the empty assertion 'Every word in language signifies something'. But that assertion is empty until we explain what the difference is between 'signifying something' and 'failing to signify something'. For if the difference intended has to be explained by saying that to signify something is to be a real word as opposed to a nonsense-word, our assertion becomes 'Every (real) word is a real word'. As things stand 'signify' does no more work than does 'modify' in the analogous case Wittgenstein appeals to in *PI* 14.

In *PI* 15 Wittgenstein introduces proper names into the language-game of *PI* 8. He does not discuss the implications of this, however, until *PI* 41ff. His point in *PI* 15 seems to be that the most straightforward case of a sign signifying something is in the relation of a proper name to the individual which bears it, where the name is physically attached to the bearer. It might be scratched on it or attached on a label. There are obvious extensions of this. But the use of 'signifies' in 'Every word in language signifies something' is so extended that the word does not obviously mean anything in that sentence.

According to the picture which Wittgenstein is criticizing, the colour samples which are used in the language-game of *PI* 8 will stand to colour words in the way that objects stand to words which mean them. Now a colour sample of red is not a word. And that might incline us to suppose it was something outside language which, in the language-game of *PI* 8, is the meaning of the word 'red'. Wittgenstein wants to say that the colour sample, although not a word, is used as part of the language. It is something which it looks as if it *had* to exist for the word 'red' to be used meaningfully in the language-game of *PI* 8. It is what the word 'red' means in that language-game, according to the name-object picture of meaning. In saying that we should reckon the samples as among 'the instruments of the language' (*PI* 16), Wittgenstein is turning his back on the 'realist' implications of this 'picture'. These are explored later. (*PI* 45–49) In *PI* 16 Wittgenstein gives notice of what he is to explain more fully in *PI* 50.

Wittgenstein emphasizes, in this section we have been looking at, the diverse functions which words have, even in simple language-games. He likens words to tools. It is no more helpful to say that every word *signifies* or stands for something than it is to say that all tools *modify* something. Such remarks are only attempts to gloss over the diverse functions or uses which words and tools have. At the same time Wittgenstein is not putting forward a theory as to the kinds of word there are. Here too, in *PI* 17, he uses the analogy with tools. Just as we might group tools in different ways depending on the aim of the classification—we might, to suggest an example, group together all tools that needed to be sharpened, thus putting chisels in the same group as the lawn-mower—so we group words in different ways. Words are not, Wittgenstein seems to be implying, to be taken as of essentially distinct kinds

Logic.

just because they are not essentially of the same kind. There is no more justification for the one kind of essentialist view than there is for the other.

This emphasis, both on the diversity of the units of language—the open-endedness of any list we might try to make of the different kinds of unit there are—and on the impossibility of identifying certain kinds of unit as essential, is continued in Wittgenstein's discussion of sentences in *PI* 18–25. Here he is partly concerned to attack the view that humans *think* in certain ways and hence that, despite the differences that appear on the surface, language has an underlying structure. That view would have the consequence that 'Slab!' is somehow incomplete and that we need to add something to it in thought. But, Wittgenstein insists: 'The sentence is 'elliptical', not because it leaves out something that we think when we utter it, but because it is shortened—in comparison with a particular paradigm of our grammar.' (*PI* 20, para. 2) In the *Tractatus* Wittgenstein had emphasized how complicated the tacit conventions were on which understanding everyday language depended. (*T* 4.002) He did not claim that thought had to make the adjustment between the apparent form of certain propositions and their logical form. But something like that seems to be required if the picture theory is to be an account of what everyday language is essentially like. We need to make up in thought for what is missing in our words. Nor do we have to be logicians to do this. Our ability to do it may be likened to our ability to speak without knowing how the individual sounds are produced. Having taken the view that a sentence is a '*combination* of names', one is obliged to hold that a sentence (like 'Slab!') which appears to consist of only *one* word is elliptical. It is not, however, that it is essentially a shortened version of 'Bring me the slab!' On the contrary, our judging it to be elliptical reflects what we happen to accept as the standard form of an order.

You may have noticed how Wittgenstein sometimes makes use of an analogous case which is not controversial in order to bring home a point. He did this in *PI* 11f. in support of his point in *PI* 10 and again in *PI* 14 in support of his point in *PI* 13. He does this in *PI* 20 by drawing attention to the fact that the structure of the Russian for 'the stone is red' is 'stone red' and asks 'do they feel the copula to be missing in the sense, or attach it in *thought*?' If we took English grammar as our paradigm, as exemplifying in a standard-setting way what the structure of a sentence really is like, we may be inclined to answer 'Yes, they must do.' This is the wrong answer. But the temptation to say it is deep-seated. In the *Philosophical Grammar* Wittgenstein refers to a French politician who once said that it was a special characteristic of the French language that in French sentences words occurred in the sequence in which one thinks them. If your first language is not French that will strike you as comical. Whereas it is very natural (to us) to think that the Russians have to compensate for the lack of the copula ('is') in hearing and using sentences with the structure 'stone red'. Wittgenstein's own comment on the example of the French politician is very relevant here:

> The idea that one language in contrast to others has a word order which corresponds to the order of thinking arises from the notion that thought is an essentially different process going on independently of the expression of the thoughts. (*op. cit.*, p. 107)

The purpose of such examples is to bring home the point that there isn't something lying beneath the surface of language—an order of thought which analysis needs to dig out. It is a point about the nature of logic on which Wittgenstein has a good deal more to say in *PI* 89–115. Logic is not concerned with some underlying structure but with 'something that already lies open to view'. (*PI* 92) The multiplicity of language-games to which Wittgenstein refers in *PI* 23 is open to view. Logic is not concerned, of course, merely with noting such diversity. 'We want to establish an order in our knowledge of the use of language; an order with a particular end in view; one out of many possible orders; not *the* order.' (*PI* 132) The idea that there is, if only we could discover it, something we might call 'the order of thinking', the final analysis of a proposition, or the structure of language, is not easily dislodged. It is not refuted by mentioning that there is a tendency to regard our own language as 'logical' in a way that other languages are not. But it may lose something of its charm.

Before going on to the next section you should read the remainder of *PI* 8–25. I have glossed over the details of some passages where I have judged that you will be able to work out the point of Wittgenstein's remarks for yourself. My remarks are intended to help you do this, not to make reading of the text unnecessary. Later on in the course you may come back to passages which I have not emphasized, passages you may conclude are important ones. Do not be surprised at this.

2.3 NAMING AND OSTENSIVE DEFINITION (*PI* 26–37)

In what I had to say about *PI* 5–6 I made little of Wittgenstein's distinction between ostensive *teaching* and ostensive *definition*, and at that stage it may not have been altogether apparent to you what the import is of the distinction between *training* and *explanation*. But in *PI* 26–37 Wittgenstein returns to a discussion where these distinctions are relevant. I would like you now to read *PI* 5–6 again and then go on to *PI* 26–32, at the end of which Wittgenstein sums up his objection to Augustine's account of the learning of human language. Make a note of your answers to the following questions:

(a)   What is the difference between 'ostensive teaching of words' and 'ostensive definition'?

(b)   What is the relevance of this distinction to the view that the meaning of a word is the object for which it stands and of which it is the name?

If you find (b) difficult you should find it helpful to consider the difference between how Wittgenstein says (*PI* 6) that children are taught the language-game of *PI* 2 and what he says about Augustine in *PI* 32. The criticisms we discussed, in the previous section, of the idea that thought is an essentially different process going on independently of the expression of the thoughts are also pertinent.

(a)   Both ostensive teaching and ostensive definition involve pointing to an object, uttering a word and thereby establishing an 'association' between the word and the thing. But an ostensive definition involves an *explanation of the meaning* of a word. It is the 'correlate' (*PI* 27) of asking something's name, i.e. it is given in answer to the question 'What is *that* called?' by saying '*That* is called...' and a name or label is introduced to the questioner. This is a language-game 'on its own' but not one, as so far described, in which the names or labels introduced are used. We might imagine it being played between a mother and her pre-school child, in which the child brings objects such as crayons and bricks, asks, and is told, what they are called. This language-game is one which is *preparatory* to the child's use of the words 'crayon', 'brick', and so on. (cf. *PI* 26) But it already presupposes that the child has *some* language. It can *ask* what these things are called.

For these reasons ostensive *definition* could not be used to introduce a child to 'block', 'pillar', 'slab', 'beam' in language-game *PI* 2, not if these words comprise the whole language of the tribe to which the child belongs. Not merely can the child not 'as yet *ask* what the name' of something is, as Wittgenstein says in *PI* 6, but no one *in that tribe* can do so. Ostensive definition is not a possibility provided for in their language as it is conceived in *PI* 6. Nonetheless the children of that tribe do learn language and pointing to objects forms an important part of teaching it to them. It is not, however, a question of explaining the words to them but rather of training them in their use. They are 'brought up to perform *these* actions, to use *these* words as they do so, and to react in *this* way to the words of others'. (*PI* 6) Their understanding of these words, their knowledge of what the words mean, does not consist in the fact that images are evoked. It consists, amongst other things, in their knowing what to do when 'Slab!' (or whatever) is called. It consists in something they have been trained to do. That is why, with the *same* ostensive teaching and a *different* training, understanding these words would consist in something different. The words would *mean* something different.

For an example of this difference we should need to imagine that these objects pointed to might play a very different role in the lives of our tribe. We should need to think of them as being other than materials out of which some building can be constructed. We might imagine stones of such different shapes being grouped—either naturally or by human intent—together on the top of a hill. The tribe we have been considering might, perhaps, see this collection of stones as a quarry. But another tribe might view it differently. They might see these stones as in some way representing the spirits of the dead—different individual spirits, perhaps, or different kinds of spirit. We might imagine that, by the sheerest coincidence, this second tribe teach their young which is which by pointing and using the very *same* noises in connection with the same *objects*. The ostensive teaching would in that case be identical—the same objects pointed to and the same sounds uttered. I hesitate to say that the same *words* are used. There is a Greek word which is pronounced 'allah' but it is not the same *word* as the Arabic for God ('Allah'). The Greek word means 'but'. We might imagine, nonetheless, that in our case the tribes are distantly connected and that it is no coincidence that the ostensive teaching of 'slab', 'pillar', etc. is the same. Even here, however, the meaning of the words—though we would be inclined to say they are the *same words*—is different. It is different because the training in the use of the words is quite different. In one tribe, when 'slab' is uttered on the hill-top, one of the stones is picked up and brought to the utterer. In the other tribe, when 'slab' is uttered, some act of piety is performed in relation to one kind of dead spirit. This latter language-game is, of course, much more complex. We could not imagine it as the language of a whole tribe. There are indeed difficulties enough in imagining the language-game of *PI* 2 as 'the whole language of a tribe'.[1] This does not, however, affect the point that with the different training each tribe has in connection with the word 'slab' the word has a different meaning.

[1] Rush Rhees, in his paper, 'Wittgenstein's Builders' (*Proceedings of the Aristotelian Society*, 1959–60), suggests that it is not possible to think of such a language, i.e. 'to imagine that they spoke the language only to give these orders on this job and otherwise never spoke at all'. (*Discussions of Wittgenstein*, Routledge, 1970, p. 76.)

(b)   The view that the meaning of a word is the object for which it stands and of which it is the name accords to ostensive definition a fundamental role in teaching language. Wittgenstein does not deny that ostensive definition does have *a* role in teaching language. It 'explains the use—the meaning—of the word when the overall role of the word in language is clear'. (*PI* 30) But to suppose it is through ostensive definition that meaning is given to words is to suppose that thought already accomplishes what is necessary to understanding such definitions. Wittgenstein wants to say that some linguistic competence is, so to say, a prerequisite for understanding an ostensive definition. Augustine, he claims, represents the child who has not learnt to *speak* any language as though he had already accomplished these prerequisites in *thought*. It is as though the child already had a language, only not this one, a language in which it could 'talk to itself'. (*PI* 32) Learning language, on such a view, would be analogous to learning a *second* language into which our thoughts can be translated.

Against this view Wittgenstein wants to say that part and parcel of learning language is being trained to respond in certain ways. Learning a language-game involves learning how to use new words through being inducted into a practice. Before someone can understand the ostensive definition 'This is called the "king"' in the context of chess, he needs to know about the game. Otherwise he will not know what is being distinguished from what or the point of distinguishing them. (See *PI* 31.) If we are not suitably prepared we will easily misunderstand an ostensive definition. Ostensive definition does not carry the weight which is put on it by the view that the meaning of a word is some object of which it is the name.

There are many aspects to the view that there is an order of thought prior to that of language and without which language would not be possible. It expresses itself equally in the view that the language in which we communicate with one another is peripheral to the real business of thinking and in the view that it would be possible to construct a language which could only be understood by one person. Both of these views entail the primacy of ostensive definition over all other means of teaching language. The first sees learning language as learning the marks or noises which are conventionally used to express certain ideas. But the ideas were there already. On that view the child who knows no langugage may already have everything except the knowledge of certain conventions, rather as a tourist in a foreign country might only need a phrase book to be able to say what he wants to say. It is a short step from that view to the view that someone could have a language for his own benefit, which could not be understood by anyone else. To make that step it is sufficient to deny that the objects with which one person has acquaintance are the same as those with which anyone else can be acquainted. The ostensive definition would then be 'private'.

These aspects of the idea that thought has a primacy over speech are ones Wittgenstein returns to later in the *Investigations*. He rejects the view that language is or might be essentially private (*PI* 243–280) as well as the idea of a 'private ostensive definition'. (*PI* 38of.) These and other aspects of the view that thought has a primacy over speech will be covered by Godfrey Vesey in Units 16–19 and by Oswald Hanfling in Units 20–22. Here I want to emphasize that Wittgenstein turns this traditional view on its head. That, I think, is the force of his remark: 'We are talking about the spatial and temporal phenomenon of language, not about some non-spatial, non-temporal phantasm.' (*PI* 108) Wittgenstein himself talks of the need to turn 'our whole examination round'. Instead of supposing that the essence of language lies *beneath* its surface and that logic is concerned with the essence of thought, we are to concern ourselves with what lies *on* the surface, what lies 'open to view'. (*PI* 92) 'The philosophy of logic speaks of sentences and words in exactly the sense in which we speak of them in ordinary life when we say e.g., "Here is a Chinese sentence", or "No, that only looks like writing; it is actually just an ornament" and so on.' (*PI* 108) The roots of the inclination to say that this is wrong stretch wide and deep in philosophical thinking. Wittgenstein recognized this. That is why the discussions of *PI* 18–24 and *PI* 26–32 belong together. The discussion of *PI* 25 is, I am inclined to think, something of a 'bridge passage' between them. The temptation to say that animals do not talk *because* they do not think is another aspect of the temptation to suppose that most of what is accomplished in language has been accomplished before a vocabulary was acquired.

2.3.1   THE *TRACTATUS* AND OSTENSIVE DEFINITION

Of the discussions in *PI* 1–137 none seems further removed from the *Tractatus* than that on ostensive definition. Not only is there no mention of ostensive definition in the *Tractatus*, but questions as to how language is taught were not then seen by Wittgenstein as central to his concerns. Insofar as such questions are touched on, the *Tractatus* account seems actually to preclude saying that 'names' or 'primitive signs' are introduced by ostensive definitions. For these are explained by means of 'elucidations' and elucidations are not definitions but 'propositions that contain the primitive signs'. (*T* 3.263) Wittgenstein insisted that a name has a meaning only 'in the nexus of a proposition'. (*T* 3.3) He cannot therefore have consistently allowed that the meaning of a name could be given by simply saying ' "N" means *this*' and pointing to what the name stands for. For, if that could be done, it would imply that 'N' had a meaning apart from its occurrence in the nexus of a proposition.

For these reasons it has been widely supposed, by commentators on the *Investigations*, that the discussions of ostensive definition are in no way directed against the *Tractatus*. If that is so, then it might seem that these early sections of the *Investigations* are, after all, as much taken up with criticism of Augustine for his own sake as on account of his intellectual affinity with the author of the *Tractatus*. I do not believe that this is so. Indeed I think there is evidence which makes the question of what these discussions of ostensive definition have to do with the *Tractatus* one which cannot be side-stepped. This evidence consists in some remarks Wittgenstein made in criticism of his earlier thought:

(a)   Wittgenstein, in the *Philosophical Grammar*, expressly links the *Tractatus* view of meaning (*Bedeutung*) with Augustine's philosophy of language:

> The concept of meaning I adopted in my philosophical discussions originates in a primitive philosophy of language.
>
> The German word for 'meaning' is derived from the German word for 'pointing'.
>
> When Augustine talks about the learning of language he talks about how we attach names to things, or understand the names of things. *Naming* here appears as the foundation, the be all and end all of language. (Part I, Sect. 19)

(b)   A few years earlier, in his discussions with Waismann, Wittgenstein had said:

> Logical analysis and ostensive explanation were unclear to me in the *Tractatus*. I thought at the time that there is a 'connection between language and reality'. (*Wittgenstein und der Wiener Kreis*, pp. 209f.)

In this second passage Wittgenstein, as I understand him, is alluding to the realist view of meaning of the *Tractatus*. Names or 'primitive signs', which admit of no further account or analysis, stand for simples. These simples or 'objects' can only be named and this 'naming' might well be regarded as 'the foundation . . . of language':

> Objects can only be named. Signs are their representatives. I can only speak *about* them: I cannot *put them into words*. (*T* 3.221)

Wittgenstein's discussion of ostensive definition leads, as we shall see, directly into a discussion of this aspect of the *Tractatus*. In this discussion of simples there is no doubt that Wittgenstein's remarks are directed towards the *Tractatus*, indeed to his earlier belief in a 'connection between language and reality'. That belief was one Wittgenstein came to regard as involving an unclarity about 'ostensive explanation'. Our present problem is to understand how this manifests itself in the *Tractatus*.

Notice, in the first place, that the unclarity is said to be about 'ostensive explanation', not specifically about ostensive *definition*, which is only one kind of explanation of the meaning of a word and perhaps only one kind of *ostensive* explanation. It does not follow, that is to say, from the fact that the 'elucidations' referred to in *Tractatus* 3.263 cannot be ostensive *definitions* that they are not ostensive explanations of some kind. It might be that we learn the meanings of 'primitive signs' by hearing them used in propositions. An 'elucidation' might be a proposition used in the presence of the objects 'meant' by the names it contains, which both puts something forward as true and shows what those primitive signs mean. This seems, incidentally, to be the view of Augustine quoted right at the outset of the *Investigations*. He is quoted as saying: 'as I heard words repeatedly used in their proper places in various sentences, I gradually learnt to understand what objects they signified'. (*PI* 1) It seems clear, from the context, that Augustine means to imply that this repeated use of words 'in their proper places in various sentences' is done in the presence of the objects these words signify. If Wittgenstein meant something similar by his 'elucidations' this would explain how he could have written *Tractatus* 3.263 with no apparent expectation that his readers might take it as a paradox:

> The meanings of primitive signs can be explained by means of elucidations. Elucidations are propositions that contain the primitive signs. So they can only be understood if the meanings of those signs are already known.

Wittgenstein seems to have come to the view that there is a difficulty with this view, that it does make it mysterious how people do actually manage to catch on. But this difficulty arises equally, no matter whether the elucidations are taken to be themselves propositions or definitions. Either way the possibility of succeeding with such elucidations seems to depend on the learner already having *some* language. This is indeed just the point made against Augustine in the *Investigations*:

> Augustine describes the learning of human language as if the child came into a strange country and did not understand the language of the country; that is, as if it already had a language, only not this one. Or again: as if the child could already *think*, only not yet speak. And 'think' would here mean something like 'talk to itself'. (*PI* 32)

The *Tractatus* also requires that, before we learn language, we must already be prepared in thought so that propositions *can* 'elucidate' primitive signs for us. I think that means that ostensive explanation is required, in the *Tractatus*, to accomplish for those who as yet have no language what it can only do for those who already have language. If that is so, then the emphasis on *training in* language over against *explanations of* language which we meet up with in these early sections of the *Investigations* (e.g. *PI* 6) may be taken as corrective of the *Tractatus* account of 'elucidations'.

There is a passage in the *Philosophical Remarks* (1929–30) which seems to do just this. Notice how the second sentence echoes *T* 3.263:

> If I explain the meaning of a word 'A' to someone by pointing to something and saying 'This is A', then this expression may be meant in two different ways. Either it is itself a proposition already, in which case it can only be understood once the meaning of 'A' is known, i.e. I must now leave it to chance whether he takes it as I meant it or not. Or the sentence is a definition. Suppose I have said to someone 'A is ill', but he doesn't know who I meant by 'A', and I now point at a man, saying 'This is A'. Here the expression is a definition, but this can only be understood if he has already gathered what kind of object it is through his understanding of the proposition 'A is ill'. But this means that any kind of explanation of a language presupposes a language already. And in a certain sense, the use of language is something that cannot be taught, i.e. I cannot use language to teach it in the way in which language could be used to teach someone to play the piano.—And that of course is just another way of saying: I cannot use language to get outside language. (Sect. 6)

We can see, then, that the possibility of Wittgenstein's being unclear about 'ostensive explanation' in the *Tractatus* is quite compatible with his rejection of the idea that the primitive signs or names can be individually introduced apart from their occurrence in propositions. It is quite compatible with allowing, therefore, that there is no place in the *Tractatus* for ostensive *definition* that his 'elucidations' were propositions which afforded ostensive explanations. If this is so—and there is some reason to think it is—then what Wittgenstein has to say about ostensive definition may be seen as relevant to the *Tractatus*. For the difficulty, as the passage from the *Remarks* brings out, is the same.

2.4 NAMES AND SIMPLES (*PI* 38–47)

We left the text of the *Investigations* at *PI* 32 and I suggest that, for the time being, you should pass over *PI* 33–37. It continues the discussion of ostensive definition and contains some valuable remarks about the relation between pointing and meaning. The discussion of ostensive definition extends right into the passage I would like you to study now, *PI* 38–46. This passage moves, however, on to the related topic of names and simples and concludes with a quotation from Plato's *Theaetetus* in *PI* 46. You will see that Wittgenstein identifies his 'objects' as *primary elements* in the sense spoken of

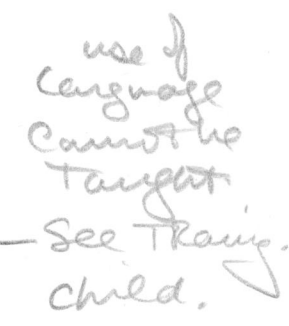

by Plato. It may help you to understand the Plato passage to look at a short passage from the *Philosophical Grammar* in connection with it. Here is that passage:

> 'In a certain sense, an object cannot be described.' (So too Plato: 'You can't give an account of one but only name it.') Here 'object' means 'reference of a not further definable word', and 'description' or 'explanation' really means: 'definition'. For of course it isn't denied that the object can be 'described from outside', that properties can be ascribed to it and so on. (I, Appendix 3, p. 208)

When you have read *PI* 38–46 and this short extract from the *Grammar* I would like you to make a note of your answers to the following questions:

Simples :
Particulars

(a)   What views of Russell and Wittgenstein in their 'Logical Atomism' period can you identify as under discussion in *PI* 38–46?

(b)   What objections are raised in these sections to the view that a word has no meaning unless there is something which corresponds to it?

(a)   *PI* 38 is strikingly reminiscent of Russell and it is evident—particularly in view of his being mentioned later in the discussion (*PI* 46)—that Wittgenstein does have Russell in mind. Russell had written: 'The only words one does use as names in the logical sense are words like "this" and "that".' (*RLA* 56, *LK* 201) The remarkable act of mind involved in staring at an object and repeating its name (or even the word 'this' innumerable times), which makes naming look like 'a baptism of an object' (para. 4), was indeed described as such by Russell. Talking about naming a dot in front of us, he said: ' "This" will do very well while we are all here and can see it, but if I wanted to talk about it tomorrow it would be convenient to have christened it and called it "John".' (*RLA* 55, *LK* 200) However, Russell's objections to what is ordinarily called a name are not those mentioned in *PI* 39. His objection to saying that 'Socrates' is a name is that a name, 'in the narrow logical sense of the word whose meaning is a particular, can only be applied to a particular with which the speaker is acquainted'. (*RLA* 56, *LK* 201) A name is 'merely a means of pointing to the thing' (*RLA* 103, *LK* 245) and can only be understood by those who know what it is applied to. In the case of things with which I am not acquainted I can only offer descriptions. Things I am not acquainted with *include* things which do not exist and perhaps constitute all those things concerning which the question of existence can be meaningfully raised, whose existence it is possible to affirm or deny. I cannot meaningfully give something a logically proper name and then say 'This exists' or 'N exists' where 'N' is a name. (Wittgenstein comes on to this view in *PI* 58.) With this qualification, however, we may note that while, on Russell's view, things with which we are not acquainted cannot be named, there is no objection to our describing things with which we are acquainted. Instead of calling the red dot in my visual field 'John' I could refer to it by the definite description 'the red dot in my visual field'. Thus Russell may be taken to restrict the use of names to entities whose existence is *certain*, with the *proviso* that, in any expression of that certainty, these entities are referred to by definite descriptions.

It may seem from this account that it would be wrong to identify Russell's 'individuals' or 'particulars' as primary elements. But in doing so Wittgenstein is not, to judge from the passage I quoted from the *Grammar*,

Russell

denying that it is possible to describe such elements 'from the outside'. A description 'from the inside' would, it seems, be a definition. And with this Russell can agree. What ordinarily pass as names are, to him, really disguised descriptions. And so we can, in Russellian terms, give a definition of 'Socrates' from the 'inside'. Its meaning is given by saying that 'Socrates' is 'the teacher of Plato' or 'the philosopher who drank hemlock' or whatever. But with a real name—a logically proper name—you cannot do this. All you can do is to name it. This is clearly Tractarian doctrine, as we see at *T* 3.221:

> Objects can only be *named*. Signs are their representatives. I can only speak *about* them: I cannot *put them into words*.

In his 1924 paper on 'Logical Atomism', Russell seems to echo this passage in saying that it is of the essence of a substance that 'it can only be *named*'. (*RLA* 158, *LK* 337) Here Russell expressly follows Leibniz when he declares that it is only to simples that the logical uses of the old term 'substance' can be applied. For Leibniz substances are the true (indivisible) unities out of which everything else is composed. Russell thought too that 'what is complex must be composed of simples'. Indeed he had, in his 1917–18 Lectures, defined 'logical atomism' as the view 'that you can get down in theory, if not in practice, to ultimate simples, out of which the world is built, and that those simples have a kind of reality not belonging to anything else'. (*RLA* 129, *LK* 270) In the earlier work these simples are not only particulars but include 'qualities and relations of various orders'. But these simples are like Plato's primary elements in being the indefinables out of which, as the quotation from Plato has it, 'we and everything else are composed'. Russell restricted the term 'name' to a certain class of simples, 'particulars' or 'individuals'. He therefore rejects the view that 'the essence of speech is the composition of names'. This restriction is founded on his Theory of Types. Since that Theory is rejected in the *Tractatus* (*T* 3.33f.), it is not surprising that the term 'name' is not subject to that restriction in the *Tractatus*. It is not possible, in the terms of the *Tractatus*, to raise the question whether its 'objects' are universals or particulars.

In the passage from the *Theaetetus* there is a further striking affinity with Russell which relates to Plato's claim that nothing is possible for a primary element other than 'the bare name'. It is that we can say of a primary element 'neither that it *is* nor that it *is not*'. This, for Russell, is a corollary of his Theory of Descriptions. Fundamental to that Theory is his distinction between names and definite descriptions. As we have just seen, most of what we ordinarily call 'names' are disguised descriptions. Taking the example of *PI* 39 we may say that if 'Excalibur' were a genuine name its meaning would simply be the object corresponding to it. The word 'Excalibur' would not have a meaning unless there were such an object. Hence 'Excalibur does not exist' would be meaningless. However, 'Excalibur does not exist' *is* meaningful. It follows therefore that we can say *what* it is that does not exist. This is the complex apparently designated by some such phrase as 'the sword known as "Excalibur"'. That phrase is a definite description. Definite descriptions are 'incomplete symbols'. This means that propositions containing them may be so analyzed as to eliminate all reference to the complexes apparently meant by such descriptions. What 'Excalibur' means is 'The sword of King Arthur which was given him by Vivien' or something like that. In order to make sense of 'Excalibur does not exist' we do not have to suppose, as Meinong would have been obliged to do, that there is some non-existent entity ('Excalibur') of which this is being said. We may say something like this:

> 1 The propositional function '*x* is a sword and Vivien gave *x* to Arthur' is false for all values of the variable '*x*'.
>
> 2 The propositional function 'If *x* is a sword given by Vivien to Arthur and *y* is a sword given by Vivien to Arthur, then *x* is identical with *y*' is true for all values of the variables '*x*' and '*y*'.

In this analysis Vivien and Arthur are treated as simples. But of course 'Vivien did not exist' and 'King Arthur did not exist' are perfectly meaningful. So a fuller analysis would treat these as disguised descriptions. And so it would go on until the only referring expressions left would be names, which we could no longer include meaningfully in sentences of the form '. . . exists' or '. . . does not exist'.

Wittgenstein's remarks in *PI* 39 lend support to the view favoured by Professor Parkinson (Units 7–10, Sect. IV.5) that he had himself been led in the *Tractatus* to accept simples by some such reasoning. Russell's Logical Atomism is in this respect frankly metaphysical. Plato has Socrates say of a 'primary element' *both* that it 'exists in its own right' *and* that no determination was possible with regard to it, 'neither that it *is* nor that it *is not*'. The *Tractatus* tries to have it both ways too. 'There are objects' is nonsensical. (*T* 4.1272) It is an attempt to *say* something which can only be *shown*. Wittgenstein does not say there *are* objects. But, in reading the *Tractatus*, we are to see that such remarks as 'Objects make up the substance of the world' are, in a way, right and then discard them as nonsensical. (*T* 6.54)

My question to you at this point was a rather open-ended one. I don't expect you to have noted all of the above and you may well have noted points I have not remarked on.

(b) The attraction of the idea that the word 'this' is the only genuine name is that it can only be meaningfully used if there is something referred to by it. It can never be 'without a bearer'. (*PI* 45) But 'this', so far from being the only name, is not a name at all. We explain the meaning of a name, sometimes, by pointing to its bearer, but that is not how the meaning of the word 'this' is explained. The gesture of pointing does not accompany the use of a name as it does commonly in the case of 'this'. Meaning is not itself a form of pointing but—at least for a large class of cases—consists in the use of a word in the language. The word 'this' is used in such a way that it has to have a bearer. But, if its meaning is the use to which it is put, the meaning of 'this' does not vary depending on what it is used to refer to. The meaning of a name, however, does depend on who it is used to refer to. But it is not identical with the *bearer* of the name. For we can still use a name where its bearer no longer exists. (*PI* 40) In neither the case of 'this' nor in the case of genuine names like 'Socrates' is the meaning to be equated with the person (or whatever) referred to by the word 'this' or bearing the name.

Throughout most of these discussions Wittgenstein has been attacking the view that the meaning of a word is something it stands for. He does not deny the importance of pointing and ostensive teaching in teaching language. His point rather is that this picture of the essence of language involves a misunderstanding of the place of pointing in teaching language. One manifestation of this misunderstanding is found in Russell's willingness to admit the word 'this' as a proper name. The word 'this', on his account, means the individual it points to at any given time. The consequence of this view is that the word 'this', since it is used to refer to different individuals, is highly ambiguous. Russell indeed accepts this consequence with equanimity. (*RLA* 56, *LK* 201) The doctrine that 'the meaning of a word is its use in the language' (*PI* 43) contrasts very sharply with such an account of the meaning of 'this'. In the first place, it would follow, as we have seen, that the word 'this' does not have as many meanings as it has referents. The meaning of 'This' in 'This is red' is the same as in 'This is blue', whether or not it is the same thing referred to. The function of the word 'this' is the same in each case. The meaning of the word 'this' is not explained by pointing. Rather, learning the meaning of the word 'this' goes with being trained to use and respond to the pointing gesture. A second point of contrast lies in the fact that the use of the word 'this' in language is something which is 'open to view'. Logical analysis encourages the idea that the meaning of a word is something which is not 'open to view'. That the word 'this', as Russell puts it, 'seldom means the same thing two moments running' can be seen as the result of a more careful scrutiny of something we do not ordinarily attend to. Yet, seen from another point of view, that consequence is a *reductio ad absurdum* of the position that leads to it. That Russell did not see it this way shows how strong a hold such a picture of meaning can acquire.

It may seem to you that Wittgenstein is simply offering an alternative view of meaning and that if we adopt his point of view then taking 'this' as a name or as radically ambiguous will seem wildly implausible. This raises the question as to the sense in which Wittgenstein can be said to offer a *theory* of meaning at all. In one sense of 'theory', a philosophical theory of meaning is almost bound to be essentialist in character, i.e. bound to be an account of what language, at bottom, is like. In Units 5–6 we saw—or, at any rate, I suggested—that Russell had a theory of this kind. He expresses it provisionally in his stipulation: 'That the components of the fact which makes a proposition true or false, as the case may be, are the *meanings* of the symbols which we must understand in order to understand the proposition.' (*RLA* 51, *LK* 196) Many symbols do not fit the theory straightforwardly. For some of them the theory needs to be modified—the so-called 'logical constants' like 'not', 'if...then', 'and', 'or', etc. Others, like definitely describing phrases and what we ordinarily class as proper names, are shown to be 'incomplete symbols'. Analysis shows these not to be an embarrassment for the theory, since they do not stand for entities which are the components or constituents of facts which make statements containing them true or false. And so the account is elaborated. Wittgenstein's *Tractatus* contains a theory of this kind.

The account of meaning offered in the *Investigations* is not an alternative *theory* of meaning in the sense in which the logical positivists provided an alternative theory. It is rather what one might call an 'anti-theory'. The use of a word is, according to Wittgenstein, just what theories of meaning divert our attention from. They lead us to a view of what it is for a proposition to have 'sense' and therefore to a view of the essence of propositions. Wittgenstein was later to say of the *Tractatus* view of the essence of propositions: 'A *picture* held us captive. And we could not get outside it, for it lay in our language and language seemed to repeat it to us inexorably.' (*PI* 115) The word 'proposition' is one which, he says, needs to be brought back from its 'metaphysical' to its 'everyday' use. (*PI* 116) I think he would have said the same about the word 'meaning'. There is no one way in which the word 'meaning' is used. The saying that 'the meaning of a word is its use in the language' (*PI* 43) is, I think, a way of summing up the correcting perspective Wittgenstein wishes to commend.

That this is so seems to me clear from the context in which this saying occurs. It is a critical context. Notice too that Wittgenstein introduces this saying as a 'definition' of the word 'meaning' which holds not for all but only for 'a *large* class of cases' in which we employ it. He concludes *PI* 43 by saying, 'And the *meaning* of a name is sometimes explained by pointing to its *bearer*.' There is *a* use of the word 'meaning' in which, asked the meaning of the word 'sepia' one might say, pointing to a sample of sepia, 'This is what the word "sepia" means'. It is the existence of such a use which makes it tempting to identify the meaning of a word with the object it signifies. Wittgenstein certainly wishes to deny that this is the only, or even the main, use of the word 'meaning'. And, even in this case, the explanation of the meaning of the word 'sepia' is also an explanation of its use. The *sample* of sepia is not, therefore, identical with the *meaning* of the word 'sepia'. The meaning of a name and its bearer do not become identical just because the meaning of the name can be sometimes explained by pointing to its bearer.

Let us return now to the text of the *Investigations*. Wittgenstein quotes Plato in *PI* 46 in much the spirit in which he had quoted Augustine in *PI* 1. In both cases there are affinities with the views of the *Tractatus*. And that is partly why they are chosen for discussion. Summing up Augustine in *PI* 1 Wittgenstein attributed to him the view that 'sentences are combinations of . . . names'. These are his words, not Augustine's. But the quotation from Plato concludes with the assertion that 'the essence of speech is the composition of names'. I do not think it is relevant to inquire further into either Augustine's or Plato's philosophy in this context. For the primary target of Wittgenstein's criticism is his own *Tractatus*. Each of Augustine and Plato, however, adds explicitly a dimension which is hinted at by the *Tractatus* but which its severe strictures on what was relevant or possible left as no more than hints. In Augustine's case that dimension is the *teaching* of language. Plato adds a metaphysical dimension. It is this metaphysical dimension which becomes prominent in *PI* 48–59.

PI 48 introduces a language-game for which the account of language in the *Theaetetus* is 'really valid'. Wittgenstein's method of considering Plato as quoted by him is thus analogous to his method of considering Augustine. Moreover, just as he voiced a critical objection to Augustine in *PI* 1 before going on to 'imagine a language for which the description given by Augustine is right (*PI* 2), so too he makes an objection to Plato in *PI* 47. It is indeed an objection to the very idea of 'primary elements' conceived of as absolute simples. The objection, which is directed equally at Russell and the author of the *Tractatus*, is that it makes *no sense* to talk of absolute simples. The objection seems linked with what has been said about meaning and use. The word 'composite' has no meaning in 'This is composite' unless what is to be counted 'simple' and what 'complex' or 'composite' has already been determined. The point of that contrast is only given within a language-game. The metaphysician concerns himself with what is truly a 'simple' (or a 'true unity') and sees our way of distinguishing 'simple' and 'composite' as not going to the roots of the matter. *PI* 47 exemplifies Wittgenstein's critique of metaphysics. 'What *we* do is to bring words back from their metaphysical to their everyday use.' (*PI* 116) That is another expression of the view that the meaning of a word *is* its use. When words are taken out of the context in which they do their normal work then language goes on 'holiday'. That is not to say that we cannot invent uses for words. But then we need to supply a context for them by inventing a language-game for them. This is what Wittgenstein does for 'simple' and 'complex' in *PI* 48.

Note on revision

Before you work further on this material, I suggest this would be a good point at which to revise the relevant sections of the *Tractatus*, *T* 2.02–2.0271 and *T* 3.202–3.23. I suggest you also re-read Units 7–10, Sect. IV.5, which deals with the interpretation of some of these passages. You will also find Units 7–10, Sect. VI.1 relevant to our next discussion.

2.5 THE METAPHYSICS OF LOGICAL ATOMISM (*PI* 48–59)

I would like you now to read *PI* 48–59, paying particular attention to *PI* 48–9 and 55–9. Please make a note of your answers to the following questions:

(a) What similarities and dissimilarities do you see between the views expressed in double inverted commas at the beginnings of *PI* 55, 57, 58 and 59 and the views expressed in the *Tractatus*?

(b) What does Wittgenstein mean when he says, in *PI* 50, para. 3: 'What looks as if it *had* to exist...is a paradigm in our language-game...'? (Compare with *PI* 104.)

(a) The quoted claim at the beginning of *PI* 57 expresses a rather Platonic view of redness as something which exists independently of the existence of red things. This is not, of course, something which the Wittgenstein of the *Investigations* was tempted to say. And, on the face of it, it is not a view expressed in the *Tractatus* either. In the first place, since the *Tractatus* rejects the Theory of Types, it cannot be interpreted as involving the view that its 'objects' are *either* simple particulars *or* simple universals. More importantly, perhaps, 'red' cannot be an element of an elementary proposition. It is a cardinal doctrine of the *Tractatus* that no two elementary propositions can be incompatible with one another. (See, e.g. *T* 1.21.) But 'This is red' and 'This is blue' are incompatible. (*T* 6.3751) So redness is not an example of a Tractarian object.

If you noted these points, you may have been inclined to deny that *PI* 57 (or, for that matter, the language-game of *PI* 48) has anything to do with the *Tractatus*. I think there are affinities in spite of these differences. For *PI* 55 and *PI* 59 do begin with a quotation which may be said to express a metaphysical commitment of the *Tractatus*. True, the *Tractatus* does not speak of 'objects' as 'indestructible'. It does, however, speak of them as 'unalterable and subsistent'. (*T* 2.0271) At the end of *PI* 59 Wittgenstein writes of a picture of reality which involves our seeing 'a whole which changes (is destroyed) while its component parts remain unchanged'. This seems to echo *T* 2.0271, where the configuration of objects is said to be 'what is changing and unstable' whereas the objects themselves are 'unalterable and subsistent'. The difference between *PI* 57 and *PI* 55 lies mainly in the fact that 'red' is taken as an example of a name.

There is a passage in the *Philosophical Grammar* (Appendix 4, p. 211) in which Wittgenstein instances 'Here is a red rose' as something which may be called an 'elementary proposition' in accordance with the usage of the *Tractatus*. In the *Grammar*, redness is admitted as an 'object', for 'object' means 'reference of a not further definable word' (p. 208) and 'red' is not further definable. I think the explanation of the divergence over whether 'red' is a name (between the *Tractatus* and the later writings) is due to the fact that one of the doctrines of the *Tractatus* which Wittgenstein first rejected was that which precluded 'red' and other colour terms from being 'names', viz. the doctrine that elementary propositions were independent of one another. This is discussed by A. Kenny in his *Wittgenstein*, Ch. 6. Once that requirement is abandoned, there is no longer the same difficulty in taking redness to be an 'object', at least for the sake of an example.

PI 58 states a view which is common to Plato (see quotation in *PI* 46), Russell (e.g. *RLA* 108, *LK* 250) and to the *Tractatus* (e.g. *T* 4.1272). We cannot say 'Red exists' because 'if there were no red it could not be spoken of at all'. This is Wittgenstein's example. But the general point, that the term '*name*' be restricted to what cannot occur in the combination 'X exists', expresses a view common to all three. Now this impossibility readily looks as if it tells us something about the nature of reality, about the nature of the primary elements. As Wittgenstein puts it:

> It looks as if we were saying something about the nature of red in saying that the words 'Red exists' do not yield a sense. Namely that red does exist 'in its own right'. The same idea—that this is a metaphysical statement about red—finds expression again when we say such a thing as that red is timeless, and perhaps still more strongly in the word 'indestructible'. (*PI* 58, para. 2)

(b)   This brings us on to the question of what is meant in *PI* 50 by Wittgenstein's remark: 'What looks as if it *had* to exist . . . is a paradigm in our language-game . . .' This remark is directed to the metaphysical overtones of Plato's remark that 'everything that exists in its own right can only be *named*'. For reasons we considered in the last section, that sort of view leads very readily to the view that such 'elements' ('objects', 'simples', 'particulars' or however they are thought of) are somehow indestructible, as if they '*had* to exist'. To the author of the *Tractatus* such a claim as 'Objects have to exist' would have been nonsensical. Yet just such a claim is hinted at by his remark at *T* 2.0271: 'Objects are what is unalterable and subsistent; their configuration is what is changing and unstable.' That picture seems to be alluded to in the remark in *PI* 50: 'everything that we call "destruction" lies in the separation of elements'. It seems as if Wittgenstein was trying to show something about the nature of language but ended up seeming to say something metaphysical about the nature of reality. This confusion is discussed in *PI* 58, para. 3. The upshot of the confusion is that the *Tractatus* account of 'objects', by a remarkable irony, is itself metaphysical. The source of the confusion is identified in *PI* 104 in the remark:

> We predicate of the thing what lies in the method of representing it. Impressed by the possibility of a comparison, we think we are perceiving a state of affairs of the highest generality.

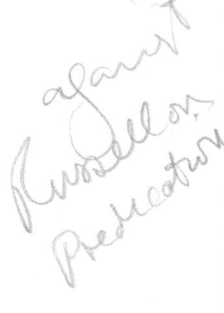

That remark is directed against the idea that logic presents 'the a priori order of the world'. (*PI* 97) At this stage we are concerned with only one aspect of that 'illusion', though a fundamental one. When we say that the words 'Red exists' do not yield a sense it looks as if we are saying something 'about the nature of red'. We predicate of the *colour red* what is really about our *use* of the word 'red'. (*PI* 58) In this sense we predicate of the 'thing' (the colour) what lies in our method of representing it, what belongs to the language-game in which we use the word 'red'. The illusion that 'we are perceiving a state of affairs of the highest generality' is a metaphysical one. One manifestation of it is the doctrine that elements 'exist in their own right'.

In *PI* 50 Wittgenstein is still discussing the language-game of *PI* 48, in which the account of primary elements given in the *Theaetetus* can be applied. An element in language-game *PI* 48, Wittgenstein wants to say, is *analogous* to a colour sample of the kind discussed in *PI* 16. In *PI* 50, para. 2, Wittgenstein has suggested that we might treat a colour sample of 'sepia' in much the way in which the standard metre kept in Paris is treated. It makes no sense to say of the standard metre either that it is or that it is not one metre long nor of the standard sample of sepia that either is or is not coloured 'sepia'. In the same way when an object is named 'R' and the name is all it has, we cannot say either that R exists or that it does not exist. Corresponding to the temptation to say that R *must* exist or, in a more disguised way, that R 'exists in its own right', there is the temptation to regard 'The standard metre in Paris is one metre long' or 'The standard colour of sepia is coloured sepia' as necessary truths. These samples are paradigms we have set up as instruments of language, i.e. we compare things with them to see whether *these* things are or are not a particular length or colour. It is by reference to the samples which are the paradigm of being one metre long or sepia that we judge things to be of that colour or of that length. They are part of the language or, at any rate, an 'instrument' of it.

I think the force of the comparison here between the absurdity of saying of an element that it exists or that it does not exist and of saying of the standard metre in Paris either that it is or that it is not one metre long may be more apparent if we consider it in terms of Russell's 'particulars'. We might imagine such a particular introduced into a language-game by being given the 'name'—going along with Russell in taking it to be one—'this'. What is referred to by 'This' in 'This is red' *has* to exist, it is tempting to say, for 'This is red' to make sense. At the same time, the combination of words 'This exists' or 'This does not exist' is meaningless. The element of necessity, which we feel attaches to the thing referred to, attaches in fact to the use of 'this' in the language-game. The connection, between 'this' and the object referred to, must be made for 'This is red' to be meaningful. It is an analogous role which samples play. If the sample is lost or destroyed then it may be that we can no longer say what is sepia and what is not, that 'sepia' loses its meaning for us. The fact, as I suppose it is, that we could still talk meaningfully about how many metres long something is even if the standard metre had been lost or destroyed shows that the language-game we play with the word 'metre' is more complicated. We have other paradigms to fall back on. But what allows me to say that my 'metre-stick', by which I measure lengths, is itself one metre long is the existence, so to speak, of a 'higher court of appeal'. In certain circumstances which we might imagine, these higher courts of appeal might disappear. This could change the status of my metre-stick. It would no longer be a *fact* about it that it was one metre long. It might then become a paradigm of being one metre long, i.e. we might say that anything which is the same length as *this* is one metre long. Saying of the metre-stick that it was itself one metre long would imply that it had been measured against itself, which is clearly absurd.

There are many other points of interest in the section of the *Investigations* (*PI* 48–59) we have been studying. I hope that by this stage you will be able to work out the significance of these for yourself. Partly for this reason I shall, as we proceed, either not comment on some passages at all or comment only partially on them.

2.6 WITTGENSTEIN'S REJECTION OF ANALYSIS (*PI* 60–64)

That there was, in Wittgenstein's early philosophy, a close connection between his commitment to analysis and his commitment to 'simples' is clear from his manner of arguing to simples from the necessity of analysis. In an entry in his *Notebooks* for 14.6.15, he had written:

> It seems that the idea of the SIMPLE is already to be found contained in that of the complex and in the idea of analysis, and in such a way that we come to this idea quite apart from any examples of simple objects, or of propositions which mention them, and we realize the existence of the simple object—*a priori*—as a logical necessity.
>
> So it looks as if the existence of the simple objects were related to that of the complex ones as the sense of $\sim p$ is to the sense of p: the *simple* object is *prejudged* in the complex.

Just as not-p ($\sim p$) is not an 'elementary' proposition but a truth-function, deriving its sense from p and being, it might be said, a construction out of p, so a complex object, to which we could refer meaningfully even if it did not exist, already presupposes simples which constitute it.[1] This is the 'picture of reality' to which Wittgenstein refers at the end of *PI* 59. It is one which leads us to see things as composed of simple parts which form 'the substance of the world'. (T 2.021) The complexes can be changed or destroyed but not the simples that constitute them. 'Objects are what is unalterable and subsistent; their configuration is what is changing and unstable.' (T 2.0271)

This 'picture of reality' has many roots and, in these early sections of the *Investigations*, Wittgenstein seems engaged in digging these out one by one. He has already dealt with the view of names. Later he is to turn to the demand for definite sense (*PI* 70–91) which, in the *Tractatus*, is said to *be* the demand for simple signs or names. (See T 3.23.) He is also to attack one of the less obvious roots, the theory of descriptions. (*PI* 79f., see Units 7–10, IV.5.1) In Sects. 60–64 his target is analysis or, at any rate, a particular conception of analysis. I'd like you to read *PI* 60–64 now, as well as a later passage, from the second paragraph of *PI* 90 to the end of the first paragraph, of *PI* 92. When you have read these passages, please make a note of your answers to these questions:

(a)   What conception of analysis is criticized in these passages? How is it articulated in the *Tractatus*?

(b)   What objections does Wittgenstein make to this conception of analysis? Do you think these are reasonable objections?

(a)   The conception of analysis attacked in *PI* 63 is one which involves thinking of the analysed form of a sentence as 'more fundamental'. This leads to the idea that there is a fundamental level of description of the world, to the idea that there are 'elementary' or 'completely analysed' propositions. (T 3.201) The idea that thre is 'a final analysis of our forms of language, and so a *single* completely resolved form of every expression' is found in the *Tractatus* remark: 'A proposition has one and only one complete analysis'. (T 3.25) The idea that there is something hidden in language which it is necessary for analysis to dig out is echoed also in the *Tractatus* by remarks about how language 'disguises thought'. (T 4.002)

(b)   One of the objections Wittgenstein makes to this conception of analysis is that, just as analysis can draw attention to aspects which would otherwise not be noticed, there are also aspects of something in its unanalysed form

[1] The connection between atomism and analysis is discussed in the radio programme related to Units 5–6, 'Russell's Logical Atomism'. See programme notes for Radio 03.

which are lost in the analysis. In *PI* 64 Wittgenstein gives an example. The flags of many countries simply consist, we may be inclined to say, of coloured rectangles put side by side. The French tricolour is one case of that. It may look to a foreigner as nothing more than a certain arrangement of blue, white and red rectangles. But a patriot will see it, one might say, as an unanalysable whole, as the French flag. We might imagine that such flags are all manufactured in Zaire and that they are only spoken of *in that context* as configurations of colours. This would be a different language-game from that in which, on occasions of national ceremony, the 'flag' is spoken of. The two language-games are related but it would be wrong to take the former as the more fundamental one or even as one which could replace the latter.

It is possible to programme a computer so that it will produce what we would see as a photograph. The language with which the computer is programmed is quite different from the language in which *we* would describe the person, place, or whatever whose likeness emerges. If you look at the cover of Units 5–6 of this course, you will see a 'blown-up' picture of Bertrand Russell. We might describe this picture very precisely by plotting the position and size of all the spots on it. But we might also describe it by talking about Russell's facial characteristics, saying that he had 'heavy eyebrows', 'a pointed nose', or whatever. There are, it seems, at least two ways of describing the same thing,[1] in this case. There are two different *forms* of description, we might say, each of which has its place in a different language-game and neither of which is reducible to the other. There are even certain elements (noses, ears, and so on) which feature in one language-game which do not feature in the other.

These ideas of Wittgenstein's involve a rejection of any view according to which there is some fundamental form of description of the world to which all other meaningful description is to be reduced. They are not simply at variance with the *Tractatus* but also with the ideas of the logical positivists, who saw the range of propositions admitted as 'protocol sentences' as determining the fundamental form of description of the world. With the abandonment of the conclusive verifiability principle the positivists' doctrine required modification. But their conception of science as a 'unified' structure is premissed upon their requirement that the propositions of science are all such that they could, in principle, be confirmed by some set of basic observation sentences. On Wittgenstein's account, observation sentences do not have the required homogeneity. What counts as 'simple', according to Wittgenstein, will be something which needs to be specified within a context. In that sense it will be a relative matter what we count as 'simple' and what not. We do not have any conception of what 'simple' is which pervades the whole of language. In describing people we commonly take the 'eye' as a 'simple' rather than as a 'complex'. We may say, in accordance with such a usage, that someone's eyes are brown. It is tempting to say that this is at least misleading, that, strictly speaking, it is not his eyes as a whole that are brown but only parts of them. In that spirit it might be suggested that the eye is a complex of 'sclera', 'pupil' and 'iris', thus:

---

[1] The phrase 'the same thing' is problematic here. For the possibility of having different ways of describing the *same* thing assumes a mode of identification common to these modes of description and therefore some common language, e.g. the word 'face' so that 'same thing' means here 'same face'. But this is not possible if there is no such common language.

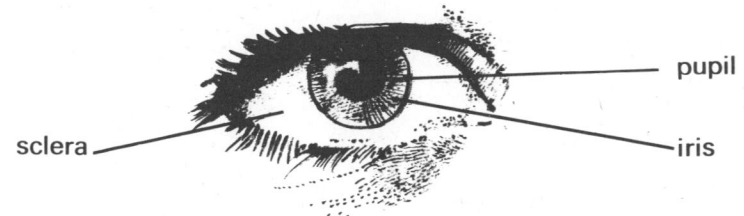

When someone says 'His eyes are brown' what he means is, it may be insisted, something exact, something wholly 'determinate'. What he means is, 'His irises are brown'. Here we might have an example where it is tempting to say that ordinary language disguises thought. For it seems that when someone says 'His eyes are brown' we understand what he means perfectly well. This is due to the existence of certain conventions which enable us to see just what he means, just in what circumstances, therefore, what he says is true and under what conditions it is false. 'The tacit conventions on which the understanding of everyday language depends are enormously complicated.' (*T* 4.002)

Once we are embarked on this quest for a more precise *expression* of what someone means, it is difficult to know where to stop. It is difficult, as Wittgenstein later points out, to settle on a *single* ideal of exactness—or, correspondingly, of simplicity—which will provide a terminal point for analysis. (*PI* 88) This is a point we shall return to.

I have chosen to divide the portion of the *Investigations* we are studying into two broad sections. In *PI* 1–64 the discussions are focused largely on questions which relate to *parts* of propositions, i.e. words, whereas *PI* 65–137 is concerned with the nature of *propositions*. Thus questions about naming, ostensive definition and simples have been to the fore in the first part. The second part, being concerned with propositions and their relation to one another, is more explicitly concerned also with the nature of logic. To some extent, however, my division is arbitrary. For it is not that the views discussed in *PI* 1–64 did not entail views about the nature of propositions. Wittgenstein, in summarizing what he takes to be Augustine's views, attributes to him not only the view that 'the individual words in language name objects' but also the view that 'sentences are combinations of such names'. (*PI* 1) Likewise, in the quotation from Plato, it is an integral part of Socrates' account of primary elements that 'the essence of speech is the composition of names'. (*PI* 46) And this is what we should expect if Wittgenstein's critical remarks are directed primarily at the sort of view he had subscribed to in the *Tractatus*. For there he had maintained that an elementary proposition 'consists of names...is a nexus, a concatenation, of names'. (*T* 4.22)

That view stands or falls with the account of names. Thus *PI* 1–64 can be seen as concerned not merely with names as the constituent parts of elementary propositions but also with the 'picture theory' put forward in the *Tractatus* about the nature of such propositions. *PI* 65–137 is equally concerned with questions about the essence of language, particularly about 'the general form of propositions'. Some of these discussions are referred to by Professor Parkinson in his treatment of what the *Tractatus* has to say on this question. I suggest you spend some time, at this juncture, revising *T* 4.5–5, *T* 5.471f. and the discussion of the general form of propositions in Units 7–10, Section VI.2.1. When you have read these passages, as well as *PI* 65 and *PI* 136, para. 1 (which Professor Parkinson discusses), please make a note of your answers to the following questions:

(a)   What is 'the thesis of truth-functionality'?

(b)   Why do you think Wittgenstein offers both a technical (*T* 6) and a non-technical (*T* 4.5) statement of the general form of propositions?

(c)   How do these statements (of the general form of propositions) relate to the thesis of truth-functionality?

(d)   How does the existence of a general form of propositions relate to the view that there must be something common to everything we call a 'proposition' (see *PI* 65) and to the view that propositions are essentially true/false?

(a)   The *thesis of truth-functionality* is the thesis that every proposition is a truth-function of elementary propositions. It is the fifth 'main' proposition of the *Tractatus*, i.e. *T* 5.

(b)   The non-technical statement of the general form of propositions, 'This is how things stand' (*T* 4.5), occurs in the context of a discussion of what it is for a proposition to have sense, i.e. be true/false. It has a sense only 'in virtue of being a picture of reality'. (*T* 4.06) If that is so then it follows, given Wittgenstein's account of such 'pictures', that 'the analysis of propositions must bring us to elementary propositions which consist of names in immediate combination'. (*T* 4.221) Another way of expressing this would be to say that given *all* elementary propositions it would be possible to construct all *other* propositions from them. There cannot therefore be a proposition whose form is not foreseeable, i.e. which could not be constructed. That is the fact which, according to Wittgenstein, proves the existence of a general propositional form. (*T* 4.5, para. 3) This raises, in turn, the problem of showing just how to state the formula for generating any proposition whatsoever out of elementary propositions. That is the problem to which *T* 6 provides the answer. Saying that the general form of propositions is 'This is how things stand' takes us no nearer to that formula. What I think it does is to express the conviction that being true/false is what all propositions have in common with one another. The need for a precise formula arises, I am inclined to think, from the fact that Wittgenstein has given a very particular account of what it is for a proposition to be true/false, i.e. have sense. It is clear from *T* 5.47f. that the general propositional form is 'the essence of a proposition', i.e. that one could say it is what '*all* propositions, by their very nature, had in common'. Its rough expression is in the statement: 'This is how things stand', its precise expression is that given in *T* 6.

(c)   If the essence of a proposition is to be true/false, and being true/false requires 'being a picture of reality', and if some propositions are not transparently pictures of reality, showing them to be so involves showing how such propositions are to be constructed out of propositions—'elementary propositions'—which *are* pictures of reality. The thesis of truth-functionality states how elementary propositions are *related* to propositions in general. It gives the clue, one might say, as to how all propositions can be *constructed* out of elementary propositions. The thesis is presupposed by *T* 6, since what *T* 6 involves is the claim that every proposition is a result of successive applications to elementary propositions of an operation which makes it a truth-function. If saying that the general form of a proposition is: 'This is how things stand' is an affirmation of the essentially *pictorial*[1] nature of the proposition, then it might be said that this affirms the possibility of constructing any proposition whatever out of elementary propositions. Wittgenstein's comment on *T* 4.5 confirms this:

> Suppose that I am given all elementary propositions: then I can simply ask what propositions I can construct out of them. And there I have *all* propositions, and *that* fixes their limits. (*T* 4.51)

There remains the very difficult problem of bringing out what propositions have in common, which Wittgenstein refers to in *PI* 65 as the very part of the investigation which gave him most headache, 'the part about the *general form of propositions* and of language'.

(d)   In *PI* 65 Wittgenstein introduces an objector who accuses him of taking the easy way out and avoiding saying what the essence of language is. The implication there is that if we knew what the general form of propositions was we would know what all propositions and hence whatever we call 'language' had *in common*. That, as we have seen, is clearly implied by *T* 5.47. *PI* 136 provides some confirmation of the suggestion that *T* 4.5 affirms the true/false character of the proposition. The force of saying that the general form of propositions is: 'This is how things stand' may be, then, that not merely are elementary propositions pictorial in character but that propositions are essentially pictorial, i.e. that we can construct those that are

---

[1] The 'picture' theory of the proposition is explained in Units 7–10, Sect. IV.

not obviously pictorial out of those that are. So construed, belief in the existence of a general form of propositions is virtually indistinguishable from acceptance of the thesis of truth-functionality.

So far we have been looking at *PI* 65 for the light it throws on the *Tractatus* account of the *general form of propositions*. We have seen that *T* 6 is, in a sense, an answer to the question: What do all propositions have *in common?* or, what comes to the same thing, 'What is the *essence* of propositions?'. It is not, of course, an answer on its own. It is only an answer *given* the account of elementary propositions. That is why Wittgenstein can say, at the beginning of *PI* 65, that he is about to say something about 'the great question that lies behind all these considerations'. The phrase 'all these considerations' may, I believe, be taken to refer back to the whole of *PI* 1-64, for throughout Wittgenstein has been concerned with a particular 'picture' of the essence of human language. The complaint he imagines someone voicing agsinst him is that he avoids the hard issues by insisting only on the diversity that exists in the use of language. The hard question, it may be objected, arises from the fact that, in spite of all this diversity, we call various activities 'language-games' or uses of 'language'. And surely, it is implied (by the objector), there has to be something common to these activities, otherwise they would not all be called 'language'. To this objection Wittgenstein replies that 'these phenomena have no one thing in common which makes us use the same word for all'. Nonetheless they are '*related* to one another in many different ways'. His view, which we shall consider in the next section, is that it is in virtue of these relationships that we call them all 'language'. This view involves a rejection of the idea that there must be a general form of propositions.

3.1 AN ALTERNATIVE TO ESSENTIALISM (*PI* 65-91)

In *PI* 65 Wittgenstein voices an objection which is expressed from the standpoint of the *Tractatus*. According to the imaginary objector, there *must* be something common to what we call 'propositions' etc. which makes us use the same word for all. The objector implies that this common element or essence of propositions is something which does not lie on the surface of language but is rather, as Wittgenstein later puts it, something 'that lies within, which we see when we look *into* the thing, and which an analysis digs out'. (*PI* 92) This objection expresses a standpoint often.referred to as 'essentialism'. The word 'essentialism' is not just a label for the views of the *Tractatus*, though such a passage as *T* 5.44ff. brings out the *Tractatus*' commitment to such a view. As we shall see, essentialism in the *Tractatus* is connected with a particular view of the nature of logic, and the alternative to essentialism presented in *PI* 65ff. is part and parcel of the alternative view of logic presented in *PI* 92ff.

Essentialism, however, thought of simply as the idea that there must be some common element, in all cases where we apply a general term, which underwrites our use of that term for all these cases, is a view which often has quite different roots. That this is so is shown by the fact that what Wittgenstein wrote in *PI* 65ff. has variously been taken either as a solution to the problem of universals or even as a new theory of universals.[1] It is quite

---

[1] See, respectively, two papers in *Wittgenstein: The Philosophical Investigations*, ed. G. Pitcher, Macmillan Papermac, 1968: Renford Bambrough's 'Universals and Family Resemblances' (pp. 186ff.) and Haig Khatchadourian's 'Common Names and "Family Resemblances"' (pp. 205ff.)

possible that you are already familiar with the substance of PI 66–69 from the context of such a discussion. This passage can reasonably be taken as having a bearing on certain views about universals. But to suppose that, in this passage, Wittgenstein is putting forward a 'family-resemblance' *theory* as an alternative to 'common-element' theories of universals would be quite wrong. That is the sort of error which we may be led into if we take the *Investigations* to be 'only an album' and therefore ignore the context of Wittgenstein's remarks. There are essentialist views of universals which cannot be right if what is said in PI 66–69 is true. But we can tell from the *context* of PI 66–69 that it is designed to explain how we can use the word 'language' (or 'language-game') and the word 'proposition' without supposing that there is an essence of language. It would have been quite inappropriate for Wittgenstein to have digressed at this stage into advancing a theory to the effect that, say, *everyday terms* are all applied to things in virtue of 'family resemblances' between those things and in spite of there being nothing common to them. As we shall see, there is no such digression. Wittgenstein is concerned with answering the objection voiced in PI 65.

3.1.1 GAMES AND 'FAMILY RESEMBLANCES' (PI 66–69)

Having used language-games in his discussion of accounts of the essence of language, it is appropriate that Wittgenstein, challenged for his account of why all these phenomena are called 'language', should reply with an account of the word 'game'. At the outset he had likened Augustine's account of the essence of language to an account of what a game is:

> It is as if someone were to say: 'A game consists in moving objects about on a surface according to certain rules...'—and we replied: You seem to be thinking of board games, but there are others. You can make your definition correct by expressly restricting it to those games. (PI 3)

The force of the objection that Wittgenstein takes the easy way out might be expressed in terms of this analogy by objecting: 'It is all very well to say: "You seem to be thinking of board games, but there are others." That leaves unanswered the (hard) question as to why they are all called "games".'

I would like you now to read PI 66–69 and make a note of your answers to the following questions:

(a)   Supposing somebody claims of an activity people have not previously engaged in that it is a 'game', on what basis is the question whether he is justified in doing so to be answered? Compare your answer with the one you think is implied by Wittgenstein's remarks in this passage and with the sort of basis an essentialist would look for.

(b)   What is the difficulty raised for an essentialist by PI 67, para. 3?

(c)   What is the force of the objection raised against Wittgenstein in PI 68, para. 2? Why should it be relevant to raise that objection?

(a)   An essentialist will look for a formula like 'A game is an activity engaged in by two or more people for amusement, with rules which determine who wins, etc.' He will use that formula as a basis for judging whether or not someone is justified in using the word 'game' in a new case. If he is a logical analyst, he will look for a set of necessary and sufficient conditions. He might say something like this:

'X is a game' is true if, and only if,

1   X is a competition between two or more people;
2   X is engaged in for amusement.

The basis which this would provide for assessing someone's claim in a new case that it is a 'game' is not difficult to state. If what is said to be a 'game' does not satisfy each of these conditions it is not a 'game' and if it does satisfy both of these conditions it is a game. The procedure, if the conditions are stated clearly enough, is straightforward. What is 'hard', from an essentialist point of view, however, is to state the conditions in such a way that they are not open to objection. These conditions I have given will not, in fact, do, as an account of the essence of what we call a 'game'. (1) will not do, since there are games (such as 'Patience') which involve only one person as well as games between two or more people which are not competitive, i.e. where no-one 'wins' (e.g. 'Consequences'). (2) will not do, since games may be played for financial gain, i.e. professionally, and not for amusement.

This is the type of account which Wittgenstein rejects. But, if there is nothing *common* to the phenomena we call 'games', how can we call them all 'games'? Wittgenstein's answer is that 'games' form a 'family', each member of which resembles some other members but where there is no common feature shared by all members. The way we tell that some new phenomenon is a 'game' is by its similarity to established members of the family. On such an account the boundary dividing what is within the class of 'games' from what lies outside it will not be a sharp one. We can invent variations on existing games which we will agree are new 'games'. But there may well be cases which we will not agree on. Think, for example, of the use of the word 'game' in the title of the play 'The War Game'.

(b)   *PI*67 mentions a difficulty which arises for an essentialist who tries to amend his account so as to accommodate the point that what we call 'games' or 'numbers' may be related only indirectly. He sees, perhaps, that some but not all games are 'competitive' and that some but not all games are played for amusement. He concedes, therefore, that not all games are both competitive and played for amusement. He suggests instead, perhaps, that what they have in common is being *either* competitive *or* played for amusement. But even this is not true of all cases of games. There are games, like Solitaire, which we can imagine someone playing, neither in competition with someone else nor for his own amusement, but rather to prove that he can do it or to prove that he can do it as quickly as he used to be able to do. To accommodate this type of case we might say that what games have in common is a 'disjunction' of properties: *either* they are played for amusement *or* for competition *or*, at any rate, for some purpose which is removed from concern with *production* of something valued or useful. This last clause might be mentioned to distinguish playing games from cooking, chopping firesticks, writing symphonies, and so on. But no one of these characteristics—relevant though it may be to mention them—is essential to something's being what we call a 'game'. Does it help to say that what is common to games is a *disjunction* of these characteristics? It is in reply to this kind of suggestion that Wittgenstein says:

> Now you are only playing with words. One might as well say: 'Something runs through the whole thread—namely the continuous overlapping of those fibres.' (*PI*67)

(c)   Wittgenstein's own account, however, is not free of difficulties. If it were possible to give a definition or analysis of 'game' then we would have something by reference to which we can explain the fact that we *agree*—by and large—in what we call 'games'. We would also have a basis for settling disagreements. In the absence of a definition which sharply demarcated what could be counted as 'games' and what not, it seems as if the use of the word 'game' is somewhat 'unregulated', somewhat arbitrary. This seems to be the force of the objection made in *PI* 68, para. 3. To the objection that, if what Wittgenstein says is true, then the language-game we play with the word 'game' is 'unregulated', he replies, in effect, that this is partly true, that the language-game is 'not everywhere circumscribed by rules'. The rules do not provide for every case in advance. The boundaries are not sharply defined. And, if they are not sharply defined, then there can be cases where somebody says that something is a 'game' but where the rules for the use of 'game' do not determine that what he says is 'true' nor do they determine it as 'false'. What he says, if the rules do not provide in advance for this case, does not have a clear truth-value at all, i.e. he has not said anything. From the point of view of the *Tractatus*, if the game we play with the word 'game' is not completely regulated then there is no longer any clear connection between a proposition's being *true/false* and its having *sense*.

It is at least arguable that Wittgenstein wished to retain a connection between something's being a proposition and its being true/false. We shall discuss this question in Sect. 3.4 below. It is the *Tractatus* doctrine of sense and, in particular, its corollary, that an indefinite sense is no sense at all, which is, as we shall see in the next section, abandoned in the *Investigations*. 'Am I inexact . . .', Wittgenstein asks rhetorically, 'when I do not tell a joiner the width of the table to the nearest thousandth of an inch?' (*PI* 88) My statement 'It is 39 inches wide' could be said to be true or false even although it is not determined in advance how far out I am allowed to be and my statement remain true. In this case whether my statement is true or false will depend, *inter alia*, on what the joiner is expected to do with it. That is what, in such a context, would give content to the idea of a standard of exactness.

3.1.2 THE DEMAND FOR DEFINITENESS OF SENSE (*PI* 70–91)

The discussions of *PI* 70–91 cover a number of topics which may seem at first sight to be not obviously related to one another: the Theory of Descriptions (*PI* 79), whether logic is concerned with the construction of ideal languages (*PI* 81), whether a vague concept is a concept at all (*PI* 71), whether there has to be 'a *single* completely resolved form of every expression' (*PI* 91), whether someone could know the meaning of a word without being able to say how it is used (*PI* 78), whether we can talk of rules at all if they do not cover every case (*PI* 82ff.), and others. We shall not examine all of these topics further here. Some, including the important discussion of rules, will be dealt with in later units. But the apparently disjointed character of these discussions challenges the methodological assumption I invited you to make at the outset, namely, that there is an underlying continuity in the argument of the *Investigations* and that, therefore, we should always try to place particular discussions in a wider context. If that assumption is correct, the topics will be much more closely related than they may appear at first sight.

The clue to how we should proceed is afforded by Wittgenstein's remark in his Preface that his new thoughts 'could be seen in the right light only by

contrast with and against the background of my old way of thinking'.
(*PI* p. *x*) What Wittgenstein has said about games and 'family resemblances'
in *PI* 66–69 has been in reply to a challenge from his old self that he takes
'the easy way out'. (*PI* 65) If his interlocutor in *PI* 67–69 cannot be identified
with the author of the *Tractatus*, still it is with the *Tractatus* rather than these
'new thoughts' that his sympathies lie. It would be reasonable to look back
at the *Tractatus* in order to identify the kind of vantage-point from which the
criticisms are being launched. If we can see how they give expression to an
inter-related set of doctrines we may be able to see how the discussions of
PI 70–71 belong together.

It seems, as I remarked in discussion of *PI* 68, as if one part of this set of
doctrines is the *Tractatus*' insistence that the sense of a proposition be
'determinate'. Let us then look at the passage in the *Tractatus* where this is
mentioned, *T* 3.23–3.251. You may find it helpful to read again the first few
paragraphs of Sect. IV.5 of Units 7–10, where there is a brief explanation of
'the requirement that sense be determinate'. When you have read the
Tractatus passage I would like you to look back at the six topics I listed at
the beginning of this sub-section and make a note of those topics (from these
six apparently unconnected topics discussed in *PI* 70–91) which you think are
directly related to *T* 3.23–3.251.

T 3.23 mentions the requirement that sense must be determinate, i.e. that a
proposition only has a sense if it has a definite sense. A vague concept is one
which does *not* have a definite boundary to its range of application, which
can therefore occur only in propositions which do not have a definite sense.
In *PI* 66–69 Wittgenstein has put forward 'game' as a concept of this sort.
From the standpoint of the *Tractatus*, however, a concept with blurred edges
is no concept at all. That is the objection voiced in *PI* 71.

T 3.24 alludes to the Theory of Descriptions in the remark: 'A proposition
that mentions a complex will not be nonsensical, if the complex does not
exist, but simply false.' As we have seen, Wittgenstein accepted the Theory of
Descriptions at the time of writing the *Tractatus*. He criticizes various aspects
of it in the *Investigations* and some criticism is put forward in *PI* 79f.

T 3.25 affirms that a proposition 'has one and only one complete analysis',
and this is a view from which Wittgenstein dissociates himself in *PI* 91. He
there remarks that 'now it may come to look as if there were something like
a final analysis of our forms of language, and so a *single* completely resolved
form of every expression'. But he then goes on to make it clear that, though
it may *look* like that, it would be wrong to suppose that it *was* like that.

To see how these remarks relate together and how therefore the
corresponding discussions of the *Investigations* belong together, it may help if
we remind ourselves that Wittgenstein had not been concerned in the
Tractatus with some kind of improvement on ordinary language. Russell had
taken the *Tractatus* to be concerned with 'the conditions which would have to
be fulfilled by a logically perfect language'. (*T*, p. *ix*) For Russell ordinary
language is full of 'logical imperfections'. For instance, nearly all of its words
are ambiguous. (*RLA* 52, *LK* 197) A logically perfect language is one which
would 'show at a glance the logical structure of the facts asserted or denied'.
Wittgenstein, however, had written:

In fact, all the propositions of our everday language, just as they stand, are in perfect logical order.—That utterly simple thing, which we have to formulate here, is not a likeness of the truth, but the truth itself in its entirety.

(Our problems are not abstract, but perhaps the most concrete that there are.) (*T* 5.5563)

There is a dichotomy between ordinary language and language as exhibited by logic. But it is not a dichotomy, as with Russell, between a logically defective language, on the one hand, and a logically perfect one, on the other. It is the dichotomy between the external appearance of language and its inner nature, between the 'form of the clothing' and the 'form of the body'. (*T* 4.002) This is emphasized again in the *Investigations*, in *PI* 81 and in *PI* 98–102. It is about ordinary language that the *Tractatus* made the requirement of determinacy of sense, of which, in the spirit of the *Tractatus*, Wittgenstein remarks: 'An indefinite sense—that would really not be a sense *at all*.' (*PI* 99) This is of a piece with the remark that 'where there is sense there must be perfect order'. (*PI* 98) In one way Russell was right to say that Wittgenstein was concerned with the conditions of a logically perfect language. Only Wittgenstein thought that the propositions of everyday language, just as they stand, 'are in perfect logical order'. Thus he took those conditions to be met by ordinary language. As he puts it in the *Investigations*, 'The idea now absorbs us, that the ideal "*must*" be found in reality'. I understand a propositional sign, I use it to say something. There is a dichotomy between my sentence and what the *Tractatus* has to say about 'the logical structure of propositions'. That is something which is bridged in the 'medium' of the understanding. (*PI* 102f.) Whenever *anyone* utters a sentence and *means* or *understands* it, according to the *Tractatus*, 'he is operating a calculus according to definite rules'. (*PI* 81)

To understand the point of the discussions in *PI* 70–91 we need to understand how Wittgenstein could have believed that the propositions of ordinary language had the character he supposed them to have. In some ways the *Investigations*, because it is more concerned with what is wrong about the *Tractatus* than what is right about it, distracts our attention from what is plausible in his earlier views. It seems uncontroversial to say that a proposition is essentially true/false and that to understand a proposition is to know what is the case if it is true. A proposition must, if that is so, be either true or false. Either reality is as the proposition says it is, or it is not. There is no 'no man's land', as one might say, between these possibilities. But if there is no such 'no man's land' between these possibilities it follows that a proposition either has a definite sense or it has no sense at all.

The importance of this idea in the *Tractatus* is not at all reflected in the almost incidental reference to 'the requirement that sense be determinate' in proposition 3.23. But something of its importance to his earlier thinking is reflected in the following passage from his *Notebooks 1914–16*, p. 67f. in an entry dated 20.6.15:

1   When I say 'The book is lying on the table', does this really have a completely clear sense? (An EXTREMELY important question.)

2   But the sense must be clear, for after all we mean *something* by the proposition, and as much as we *certainly* mean must surely be clear.

3   If the proposition 'The book is on the table' has a clear sense, then I must, whatever *is the case*, be able to say whether the proposition is true or false. There could, however, very well occur *cases* in which I should not be able to say straight off whether the book is still to be called 'lying on the table'. Then—?

4   Then is the case here one of my knowing exactly what I want to say but then making mistakes in expressing it?

5   Or can this uncertainty TOO be included in the proposition?

6   But it may also be that the proposition 'The book is lying on the table' represents my sense completely, but that I am using the words, e.g. 'lying on', with a *special* reference here, and that elsewhere they have another reference. What I mean by the verb is perhaps a quite special relation which the book now actually has to the table.

7   Then are the propositions of physics and the propositions of ordinary life at bottom equally sharp, and does the difference consist only in the more consistent application of signs in the language of science?

8   Is it or is it not possible to talk of a proposition's having a more or less sharp sense?

9   It seems clear that what we MEAN must always be 'sharp'.

I have numbered the paragraphs of this passage for ease of reference. Notice that Wittgenstein here admits that ordinary *sentences* can be vague, that nonetheless what is *meant* must always be 'sharp'. This reflects a point echoed in *T* 4.002 about the complicated nature of everyday language. 'There is enormously much added in thought to each proposition and not said.' (*Notebooks*, p. 70) Considering a case just like that mentioned in para. 3, but where someone presses the point that you don't know what 'lying on' means if there are cases when you could not say straight off whether something was lying on something else or not, he remarks: 'I should say: "I *know* what I mean; I mean just THIS", pointing to the appropriate complex with my finger.' (*Notebooks*, p. 70) What is added in thought is what makes the proposition 'The watch is lying on the table' into a picture of reality and thereby gives it a determinate sense. What seems to be meant in para. 6 when Wittgenstein writes of using the words 'lying on' with a '*special* reference' is that there is something precise which is *here* meant by 'lying on'.

What in the ordinary way of things needs to be added in thought can only be discovered when it is revealed how it is possible for a proposition to express something, truly or falsely, about reality, i.e. how a proposition has a definite sense. This is what is revealed by analysis. That is why, in explanation of his remark that a proposition has 'one and only one complete analysis' (*T* 3.25), Wittgenstein goes on to say that what a proposition expresses it expresses 'in a determinate manner' and that this is something 'which can be set out clearly'. (*T* 3.251) In this way the requirement that sense be determinate and the claim that a proposition has one and only one complete analysis are closely related in the *Tractatus*.

In an early version of the *Tractatus* Wittgenstein noted that a commitment to determinacy of sense precluded any change of mind as to what was entailed by a proposition. Any such change of mind would alter the sense of the proposition. Given the sense it has, it has certain definite consequences which are settled in advance. He wrote:

> The analysis of signs must come to an end at some point because if signs are to express anything at all, meaning must belong to them in a way that is once and for all complete.

> The requirement of determinateness could also be formulated in the following way: if a proposition is to have sense, the syntactical employment of each of its parts must have been established in advance. For example it cannot occur to me only subsequently that a certain proposition follows from it. Before a

proposition can have a sense, it must be completely settled what propositions follow from it. (*Proto Tractatus*, 3.20102–3)

From the stand-point of someone who was committed to accepting the requirement that sense be determinate as a requirement of ordinary language, it is not acceptable to say the things Wittgenstein says about the use of the word 'game'. The rules for its use do not cover every possible case in advance. It is not settled in advance that there cannot be cases where we do not know whether to say that something is a 'game' or not. The boundary between games and other things is not sharply defined. A good deal is at stake in this dispute. For, once the requirement of definiteness of sense is abandoned, the route to the demand for simples is largely cut off. There is, in that event, no longer a case for saying that language disguises thought and for emphasizing what thought needs to do to make a proposition a determinate picture of reality. It could then be said, as Wittgenstein puts it in his *Philosophical Grammar*: 'It is *in language* that it's all done.' (p. 143) But, if it *is* all done in language then the role of logic must be quite different from what Wittgenstein had formerly supposed. Logic will no longer be regarded as the essence of thought (*PI* 97) but will speak of sentences and words 'in exactly the sense in which we speak of them in ordinary life'. (*PI* 108) We shall return to these implications shortly.

I hope these remarks will make it clearer to you how the discussions of *PI* 70–91 belong together and why they should lead into a discussion of the nature of logic. I have not indicated, however, how the Theory of Descriptions fits into these discussions. So let us look more closely at a passage in which it is discussed.

3.1.3 THE THEORY OF DESCRIPTIONS (*PI* 79f.)

A philosophical analysis, such as the Theory of Descriptions, undertakes to give the meaning of some expression where it is not clear what the meaning is or, perhaps, where there is doubt as to whether it has meaning. Insofar as it is possible to analyse statements containing a particular expression those statements must have a definite sense. Thus anyone who denies that a statement has a definite sense is thereby committed to saying that it does not admit of exact analysis. The Theory of Descriptions is an analysis Wittgenstein is committed to reject once he has said that sentences can have a sense without having a *definite* sense. I suggest you now look at *PI* 79f. to see how Wittgenstein's remarks about 'Moses did not exist' differ from the kind of analysis favoured by Russell. When you have done so, ask yourself how you would answer the following questions:

(a) Is it possible, according to Wittgenstein, to state the truth-conditions of 'Moses did not exist'?

(b) Does whether 'There is a chair' makes sense depend upon whether the world goes on much as before, e.g. on the fact that chairs do not vanish and re-appear?

(a) Wittgenstein's position might be expressed in one of two ways. One is to say that there is not a clear set of truth-conditions which explains what we mean by 'Moses' since the use of 'Moses' is not fixed and unequivocal for all possible cases. The other is to say that of course you can try giving a definition of 'Moses'—an analysis of 'Moses did not exist'—but then you may find you want to alter your definition. The upshot is the same either way. You can define 'Moses' as 'the man who led the Israelites out of bondage in

Egypt' and then, if there were several leaders, you will probably want to change the definition rather than say that Moses did not exist. But it might be better to say that you cannot substitute a definite description for a proper name such as 'Moses', cannot therefore use the Theory of Descriptions to explain how 'Moses did not exist' has meaning. It is not that we have no idea in what circumstances we should say 'Moses did not exist', only that these circumstances cannot be fully specified *in advance*. It isn't clear, for instance, what things that are true of Moses are only incidentally true and what—were they false—would incline us to deny that Moses ever existed. There is not a sharp distinction between the *defining* properties of a thing and the properties it *happens* to have.

(b)   The aspect of the Theory of Descriptions which Wittgenstein is rejecting in *PI* 79 is that which takes it for granted that 'Moses' and other names which are, according to that theory, disguised descriptions, have an exact meaning and that propositions containing them have a definite sense. The point is the same as that Wittgenstein wishes to make for general terms such as 'game' and 'chair'. We manage well enough with these terms given the circumstances in which we use them. We can imagine circumstances in which we do not know what to say. It might be thought to be a defining property of a chair that you can sit on it. But supposing there was something that looked like a chair only disappeared just as people lowered themselves into it, leaving them floundering on the floor. I take Wittgenstein's point to be that in such a case we would not know whether to say it was a chair or not. The rules governing the use of the word 'chair' do not provide for every contingency. If all chairs were like this one we would no longer have the concept that we do have, of something which is supposed to bear the weight of a human body. The word 'chair' would no longer serve the function in our language that it presently does. It could, of course, serve another function. But the meaning it has would then be different. That is to say that, if the world were very different, there would not be the point there is in making the distinction we do make between what we call 'chairs' and other kinds of thing. In that sense the meaning of 'chair' does depend on the world going on much as before.

This topic is dealt with by R.M. White in his paper 'Can whether one proposition makes sense depend on the truth of another? (*Tractatus* 2.0211)', in *Understanding Wittgenstein* (Macmillan, 1974) Ch. 2. White explains why Wittgenstein, in the *Tractatus*, would have found an affirmative answer to this question quite unacceptable and how, in the *Investigations*, he had nonetheless moved towards just such an affirmative answer. White holds that Wittgenstein continued to connect a proposition's making sense with its being true/false. And that view is not brought in question by Wittgenstein's rejection of the requirement that sense is determinate. Not all possibilities are envisaged by our use of the word 'chair'. But those cases, like the fanciful one I mentioned in my answer to (b) above, where it is no longer clear what is meant by the word 'chair', are also cases where we would no longer know what is the case if 'There is a chair' is true. Wittgenstein stresses that 'Stand roughly there' may be a perfectly satisfactory explanation of where someone is to stand. That implies that 'He is standing roughly there' may have a truth-value. It does not follow from its not having a sharp sense that it has no sense at all. Its being true or false is tied to its having a sense. In the *Tractatus* it is further required that its sense must be definite or a proposition has no sense. But it is this requirement which is being rejected, in *PI* 70–91, not the connection between having a sense and being true/false.

3.2 LOGIC AND 'THE A PRIORI ORDER OF THE WORLD' (*PI* 92–108)

Wittgenstein makes it clear, in *PI* 65, that his discussion of games and family resemblances has a bearing on what he is going to say in his remarks about propositions. These take the place occupied in the *Tractatus* by his discussion of the '*general form of propositions*'. He makes it clear, in other words, that what he has to say about the word 'game' is relevant to what he will be saying about 'proposition', namely, that 'these phenomena have no one thing in common which makes us use the same word for all,—but that they are *related* to one another in many different ways'. It should come as no surprise, therefore, that he should claim, in *PI* 108, 'that what we call "sentence" and "language" has not the formal unity that I imagined, but is a family of structures more or less related to one another'. And again, in *PI* 135, he expressly relates what he is saying about 'proposition' to what he has said about 'game' and 'number' in *PI* 66–69. Thus the discussion of the essence of propositions can be said to span the whole of *PI* 65–137. It is not the only topic, of course, which is discussed in these sections. There are important discussions of the nature of logic and philosophy. These more general discussions, however, occur in the context of the discussion of the nature of propositions. That will seem less remarkable, perhaps, if we recall that Wittgenstein had once thought of calling the *Tractatus* '*Der Satz*' ('*The Proposition*').

Wittgenstein's strategy, in discussing the word 'game' before approaching that of 'proposition' directly, is in one respect similar to that adopted elsewhere. His purpose is persuasive. Philosophers are inclined to treat certain concepts such as 'proposition' as '*super*-concepts' (*PI* 97) and not to accept that the use of words like 'proposition', if they have one, must be 'as humble a one as that of the words "table", "lamp", "door"'. (*PI* 97) Philosophers have nothing theoretical at stake with the word 'game' and so there is no bar to their accepting that there is nothing common to all those things we call 'games'. On the other hand a great deal is at stake in discussions of the essence of language, propositions, truth, and so on. We want to be able to distinguish between strings of words by means of which something can be *said* about the world and strings of words which *appear* to be yet are not actually meaningful. That distinction remains for Wittgenstein a crucial one. What he rejects is that way of drawing it which depends upon a view about the essence of a proposition. His remarks are intended, in part, to show that the distinction between sense and nonsense does not require a thesis about what is essential to something's being a proposition. His aim is to get philosophers to think of words like 'proposition' in the way in which they already think of words like 'game'. It is something which may be likened to a kind of therapy. (See *PI* 133.)

In *PI* 92–108 Wittgenstein's remarks are perhaps more specific to the *Tractatus* than at any other point in the *Investigations*. These and the next twenty or so sections are marked by an unusual combination of passion and density of thought. In *PI* 92–108 he is, I think, trying to articulate what, at heart, is wrong with the *Tractatus* conception of logic and, by contrast with this, to articulate his later view. It is difficult to understand these passages because of the concentrated form in which they present some of the most profound aspects of both the thought of the *Tractatus* and the new ideas of the *Investigations*. Wittgenstein's remark, in the Preface, that his new thoughts 'could be seen in the right light only by contrast with and against the background of my old way of thinking' (*PI* p. x) is not equally true of every part of the *Investigations*. But there is no part of which it is more true than the section we are about to study.

I suggest that we begin our study of *PI* 92–108 by looking at a section in the middle of it, *PI* 98–102. My reason for suggesting that we start here is that *PI* 98 opens on a note of firm agreement with the *Tractatus*. The passage also refers back to themes we have already discussed in these units. When you have read it, several times if necessary, please make a note of how you would answer the following questions:

(a)   What point of agreement constitutes the starting-point for this discussion of the *Tractatus*?

(b)   What consequences are drawn, in the *Tractatus*, from this starting-point?

(c)   What problems, according to this passage, does drawing those consequences lead to?

(a)   That every sentence in everyday language is 'in order as it is' is a common starting-point to all periods of Wittgenstein's philosophical writing. In the *Tractatus* he is quite emphatic about this:

> . . . all the propositions of our everyday language, just as they stand, are in perfect logical order.—That utterly simple thing, which we have to formulate here, is not a likeness of the truth, but the truth itself in its entirety. (*T* 5.5563)

He goes on to say, in parenthesis, that the problems he is dealing with are not 'abstract' but 'perhaps the most concrete that there are'. That, incidentally, is the part of *T* 5.5563 explicitly referred to in *PI* 97. The question he is trying to answer is about what *actual* language must, at bottom, be like in order to accomplish what indeed it does accomplish. That everyday language is in order as it is, that 'there must be perfect order even in the vaguest sentence' is no innovation of the later philosophy. It is a cardinal doctrine of the *Tractatus*. On this point Russell seriously misunderstood and misrepresented[1] Wittgenstein's earlier thought. It is a misunderstanding which may well have led Wittgenstein to express himself, in the *Philosophical Remarks*, as follows:

> 3   How strange if logic were concerned with an 'ideal' language and not with *ours*. For what would this ideal language express? Presumably, what we now express in our ordinary language; in that case, this is the language logic must investigate. Or something else: but in that case how would I have any idea what that would be?—Logical analysis is the analysis of something we have, not of something we don't have. Therefore it is the analysis of propositions *as they stand*. (It would be odd if the human race had been speaking all this time without ever putting together a genuine proposition.)

These remarks in no way constitute an objection to the *Tractatus* but the re-affirmation of one of its starting-points.

(b)   The *Tractatus* embraces two views of everyday propositions which may appear, at first, to be inconsistent:

>   (i)   The propositions of everyday language are in perfect logical order as they are and have a wholly determinate sense:

---

[1] This point, relating to Russell's suggestion that Wittgenstein was 'concerned with the conditions which would have to be fulfilled by a logically perfect language' (*T* p. *ix*), was discussed in the radio programme, 'Wittgenstein on "simples"'. See broadcast notes for Radio 05.

(ii)   Everyday language disguises thought (*T* 4.002), therefore it is necessary for logic to bring out the real logical form of propositions (*T* 4.0031). The application of logic determines the elementary propositions into which propositions must be analysable, given that they have a wholly determinate sense. (*T* 5.557)

These views are not, in fact, inconsistent at all, but interpreters of the *Tractatus*, under Russell's influence, have tended to take (ii) very seriously and either ignore (i) or take it with a pinch of salt. Unless we take (i) just as seriously as (ii), however, we shall not see how Wittgenstein could have regarded the strict and clear rules of the 'logical structure of propositions' as 'hidden in the medium of the understanding'. (*PI* 102) But, given (i), we can, I think, see that logic and analysis do not, for most purposes, accomplish anything which is not already accomplished by ordinary-language users. Certainly logic and analysis can correct misunderstandings which ordinary language invites. But, and this is a point of continuity in Wittgenstein's thinking, it is *philosophers* who are particularly disposed to such misunderstandings. 'Most of the propositions and questions of philosophers arise out of our failure to understand the logic of our language.' (*T* 4.002) But most people are not philosophers and they manage to express themselves and communicate with one another perfectly well. Logic and its application only make explicit a process which must already take place. 'The tacit conventions on which the understanding of everyday language depends are enormously complicated.' (*T* 4.002) That is why Wittgenstein writes of the clear and strict rules of the logical structure of propositions:

> I already see them (even though through a medium): for I understand the propositional sign, I use it to say something. (*PI* 102)

The 'I' here is not Wittgenstein the philosopher but Wittgenstein, as one might say, in civilian life.

Logic, Wittgenstein writes in *PI* 97, is the 'essence' of thought. It makes explicit what thought already accomplishes. It follows from this that illogical thought is impossible and that thought itself actually makes the kind of connection between the propositional sign and the world which is required by the *Tractatus* doctrines of 'sense'. These corollaries may seem so astonishing[1] as to raise doubts as to whether Wittgenstein actually believed them when the *Tractatus* was written. Yet he seems to have embraced them quite explicitly, as the following passages indicate:

> In a certain sense, we cannot make mistakes in logic.

> ...language itself prevents every logical mistake.—What makes logic a priori is the *impossibility* of illogical thought. (*T* 5.473f.)

> If we know on purely logical grounds that there must be elementary propositions, then everyone who understands propositions in their unanalysed form must know it. (*T* 5.5562)

---

[1] Here, however, it is worth drawing attention to the fact that Wittgenstein was not alone in being tempted by the idea that illogical thought is impossible. Spinoza also took such a view: 'Now many errors consist of this alone, that we do not apply names rightly to things. For when any one says that lines which are drawn from the centre of a circle to the circumference are unequal, he means, at least at the time, something different by circle than mathematicians. Thus when men make mistakes in calculation they have different numbers in their heads than those on paper. Wherefore, if you could see their minds, they do not err; they seem to err, however, because we think they have the same numbers in their minds as on the paper.' (*Ethics*, Pt. II, Prop. LXVII Note, Everyman Edition, p. 74).

This last passage, incidentally, occurs immediately before the remark that 'all the propositions of our everyday language, just as they stand, are in perfect logical order'. It is beyond dispute that Wittgenstein regarded them as connected.

(c)   This idea, that ordinary people somehow 'see' the strict and clear rules of the 'logical structure' of propositions through the 'medium' of the understanding (*PI* 102), that they 'know' that there are 'elementary propositions', involves a highly idealized view of thought and understanding. It is the 'ideal' referred to in *PI* 101 which we feel *must* be found in reality. We do not see *how* it is found in reality, nor do we understand the nature of this 'must'. These are symptoms of a state of dogmatic confusion which Wittgenstein later puts forward as involving a 'bewitchment of our intelligence by means of language'. (*PI* 109) We are dazzled, as he puts it in *PI* 100, by an ideal and therefore 'fail to see the actual use' of language clearly. Against this Wittgenstein mentions in *PI* 99 that language is not wholly determinate with regard to sense and suggests that, nonetheless, it serves its purposes just as a fence may do which has a gap in it. It can no more be said, his remarks imply, that an indefinite sense is no sense at all than it can be said that an enclosure with a gap in it is not really an enclosure. He mentions also, in *PI* 101, that we need no more suppose that everything we call 'language' has something in common than we need to suppose that everything we call a 'game' has something in common. Rather, as he goes on to say in *PI* 108, 'what we call "sentence" and "language" has not the formal unity that I imagined, but is the family of structures more or less related to one another'. These are now familiar points. When Wittgenstein makes them he takes himself to be *describing* the actual workings of language as opposed to the kinds of *explanation* suggested by the *Tractatus*. (*PI* 109) But the root of the problem is not reached by simply drawing attention to the fact that actual language does not appear to fit a particular theory of it. The root of the problem lies in the way someone who has a view about what language *must* be like is prevented from giving due weight to reminders of what it is actually like. To that extent, the difficulties mentioned in *PI* 99 and *PI* 100 do not go to the root of the problem. That is something Wittgenstein comes closer to in *PI* 103–7.

We shall return, in Sect. 3.3, to a consideration of Wittgenstein's later views about the nature of philosophy. But I hope that you will be now be able to make something of *PI* 93–97, which deals more particularly with the way thought is idealized in the *Tractatus*. It also touches on themes which, in other places, Wittgenstein refers to by speaking of 'the harmony between thought and reality'. Let us turn to them now.

3.2.1   THE 'HARMONY BETWEEN THOUGHT AND REALITY' (*PI* 93–97)

To understand a proposition, according to the *Tractatus*, is to know what is the case if it is true. (*T* 4.024) It is arguable that Wittgenstein continued to believe this. Propositions can communicate a new sense to us by a use of old expressions and, to do this, a proposition must be '*essentially* connected with the situation' which, if it is true, obtains. (*T* 4.03) This too, it might be argued, Wittgenstein continued to believe. The possibility of saying anything, true or false, about the world implies some harmony between language, on the one hand, and reality, on the other. What is that harmony? How is it possible for a proposition to be 'essentially connected' with the situation it presents? These are questions to which Wittgenstein gave very different answers in his later philosophy from those he had given in the *Tractatus*.

According to the *Tractatus* this essential connection between a proposition and the situation it presents consists in the proposition being a 'logical picture' of that situation. (*T* 4.03) There is an 'internal relation' of depicting between language and the world which is, according to the *Tractatus*, analogous to the relation between a gramophone record, the musical idea, the written notes, and the sound waves. (*T* 4.014) This takes us into more complicated matters than can be reviewed here. You may therefore find it helpful at this stage to refer back to Units 7–10, Sections III and IV, where the 'picture' theory of the proposition is explained.

Here is a comment which Wittgenstein made on his *Tractatus* views in his *Philosophical Grammar*:

1   Like everything metaphysical the harmony between thought and reality is to be found in the grammar of the language.

2   Here instead of harmony or agreement of thought and reality one might say: the pictorial character of thought. But is this pictorial character an agreement? In the *Tractatus* I had said something like: it is an agreement of form. But that is misleading.

3   Anything can be a picture of anything, if we extend the concept of picture sufficiently. If not, we have to explain what we call a picture of something, and what we want to call the agreement of the pictorial character, the agreement of the forms.

4   For what I said really boils down to this: that every projection must have something in common with what is projected no matter what is the method of projection. But that only means that I am here extending the concept of 'having in common' and am making it equivalent to the general concept of projection. So I am only drawing attention to a possibility of generalization (which of course can be very important).

5   The agreement of thought and reality consists in this: if I say falsely that something is *red*, then, for all that, it isn't *red*. (p. 162f., cf. *Zettel* 55ff., *PI* 429ff.)

According to the *Tractatus*, the apparent gulf between a sentence and the world is one which is crossed in thought. That is how, for example, 'My brother is in America' can mean what it does mean. The perceptible sign of a proposition, such as the words 'My brother is in America', is used as a projection of a possible situation (my brother's being in America). The method of projection is by thinking of the sense of the proposition. (*T* 3.11) Thus the essence of thought, of logic, and indeed the world, must be the same. Logic, in presenting the essence of thought, presents 'the a priori order of the world'. (*PI* 97) This 'a priori order' is something which, Wittgenstein believed, must be 'common to both the world and thought'. (*PI* 97) That, of course, is a representation of the *Tractatus* belief in a harmony between thought and reality. Such a harmony is presupposed, according to the *Tractatus*, by the possibility of significant discourse, i.e. by the possibility of saying things, true or false, about the world. It is one aspect of the realist view of 'sense' adopted in the *Tractatus*. It is the fact that the world could be arranged in the way our propositions portray it as being arranged that underwrites those propositions having 'sense'.

With these considerations in mind, let us turn to *PI* 93–97. When you have read this passage, please make a note of your answers to the following questions:

(a)   What is the 'paradox' mentioned in *PI* 95? How can it *both* be a 'paradox' *and* have 'the form of a truism'? (Para. 5 of the passage just quoted from the *Philosophical Grammar* should help you to answer this.)

(b)   Why should there be a tendency 'to assume a pure intermediary between the propositional *signs* and the facts'?

(a)   The short answer, of course, is that *thought* can be of what is *not* the case. That evidently has the form of a truism but it is not evidently paradoxical. There is a paradox only if what is meant, when someone says something, is actually identified with a fact. If I say 'This book is red' what I *mean* is that this book is red. My meaning does not stop anywhere short of the fact. It seems that it cannot 'stop...short of the fact' if what I am saying is that just that situation obtains. Yet if what I mean is the fact itself, how can what I say have meaning if the book is not red? This is a problem referred to in Units 5–6, Sect. 3.1 as a problem for a realist view of meaning. It is not, however, a paradoxical consequence of the *Tractatus* but rather a paradox to which the *Tractatus* provides a solution. If the 'paradox' remains a problem, therefore, it must be because of the terms in which it is resolved in the *Tractatus*, i.e. in the account there given of how a false proposition can have 'sense'. It is this, I am inclined to think, which made Wittgenstein regard thought as something 'unique'. (*PI* 95) It is on this account that there has to be a rather special agreement between thought and reality. Without the problem of falsity there would not be the same need for a 'pure intermediary' between the propositional *signs* and the facts. If we abandon a realist view of meaning then we are left with the truism that if I say falsely that something is red it isn't red.[1] It is, I think, in opposition to such a realist view that Wittgenstein inserts the clause 'for all that' in para. 5 of the passage quoted from the *Philosophical Grammar*, as he does also in *PI* 429.

(b)   I have already indicated that the tendency to assume a 'pure intermediary' is, in my opinion, due to problems posed for a realist view of meaning by the existence of false (and therefore meaningful) propositions. The context itself, of course, suggests some connection. It is also indicated by the extensive discussion of how thought can be of what is not the case in *The Blue Book*. (*BB* 31–41) One response he mentions to the problem of falsity is that of saying that 'as the object of our thought isn't the fact it is a shadow of the fact'. There are, he goes on, 'different names for this shadow, e.g. "proposition", "sense of the sentence"'. (*BB* 32) He concludes, however, that 'we gained nothing by assuming that a shadow must intervene between the expression of our thought and the reality with which our thought is concerned'. (*BB* 41) The pursuit of such intermediaries or shadows is, Wittgenstein contends, a pursuit of 'chimeras'. (*PI* 94) In his later philosophy he is not disposed to such pursuits. We do not need any shadow of the fact that something is red to say, falsely, of it that it *is* red.

What, then, is the force of Wittgenstein's remark that, like everything metaphysical, 'the harmony between thought and reality is to be found in

---

[1] Notice that Wittgenstein stresses the word 'red'. It is important to bear in mind here that 'red' is being used as an example of a name for a simple. The problem of 'the harmony between world and thought' is posed in the *Philosophical Grammar*, p. 142, by saying: 'I can't think that something is red, if the colour red does not exist'. By contrast I *can* think 'The King of France is wise' even if there is no King of France.

the grammar of the language'? It is, I believe, closely connected with his remark that 'It is *in language* that it's all done'. (*Philosophical Grammar*, p. 143) There is nothing unique or extraordinary which 'must be achieved by propositions'. We do not need to suppose that kind of harmony between thought and reality which makes logic, as the essence of thought, metaphysical, as something which presents the a priori order of the world. The harmony is secured in the language itself. What we are inclined to predicate of the thing lies in our method of representing it. (*PI* 104) Logic, Wittgenstein now wants to say, is concerned with the kinds of feature of language which are 'already in plain view' and not something that lies beneath the surface. (*PI* 92) 'The philosophy of logic speaks of sentences and words in exactly the sense in which we speak of them in ordinary life when we say e.g. "Here is a Chinese sentence", or "No, that only looks like writing; it is actually just an ornament" and so on.' (*PI* 108)

The *Tractatus* commitment to a 'harmony' between thought and reality is a requirement, something made necessary by the account given of what it is for a proposition to have 'sense'. Wittgenstein's later comments at this point parallel, in some measure, those on the tacit commitments of the *Tractatus* to some kind of necessary existent. As he puts it in the *Philosophical Remarks*:

> What I once called 'objects', simples, were simply what I could refer to without running the risk of their possible non-existence; i.e. that for which there is neither existence nor non-existence, and that means: what we can speak about *no matter what may be the case*. (p. 72)

What looks as if it *had* to exist, is part of the language, Wittgenstein insists in his later discussions of simples. (E.g. *PI* 50, cf. Sect. 2.5 above.) Wherever we have a necessity of some kind, indeed, Wittgenstein refers this to grammar. And it is no longer the kind of logical grammar of his atomist period which he has in mind. Grammar is no longer seen as something invariant which underlies language but as something variable and shown by the surface features of language. In a metaphysical sense, then, grammar is cut off from any underlying connection with reality. It is 'autonomous'. (See Units 16–19, Sect. 2.6, for development of this point.) In another sense, however, knowledge of grammar remains knowledge of a harmony between thought and reality. Only that harmony is secured wholly on the side of language.

These are profound and difficult ideas which I can only give intimation of here. You will find yourself returning to them at later points in the course. Here we are concerned with them in the context of Wittgenstein's revolutionary views about the nature of logic. He epitomizes these to some extent in a remark made in *PI* 108: 'the axis of reference of our examination must be rotated, but about the fixed point of our real need.' This need, and the way in which it should be met, is in the foreground of Wittgenstein's discussions in *PI* 109–133.

3.3 THE 'BUSINESS OF PHILOSOPHY' (*PI* 109–133)

We come now to one of those parts of the *Investigations* to which followers and critics of Wittgenstein alike have turned for handy quotations of his general views about the nature of philosophy. And certainly Wittgenstein, in these sections, was attempting to characterize the re-orientation of philosophy which he thought was necessary. He was clearly not just concerned, in these passages, with offering an alternative view to that implied by the *Tractatus*. If you look at *PI* 116, for example, you will find him talking about 'philosophers' and the way in which they try to grasp the essence of what is meant by 'knowledge', 'being', 'object' and so on. The *Tractatus* was not concerned with knowledge or being and there has indeed been nothing about knowledge in the *Investigations* up to this point. In these two cases it is likely Wittgenstein was thinking about Plato. He had evidently read the *Theaetetus*. (See *PI* 46, *Blue Book*, p. 20.) He may also have had Augustine in mind. So these sections are not merely part of his self-criticism. Nor, however, can they reasonably be construed as the observations of a connoisseur. It seems that Wittgenstein did not study the classics of philosophy in any systematic way[1] but only what he could relate to his own thoughts. If these remarks about the nature of philosophy were generally right, his hitting the nail squarely on the head would owe something to good fortune. If they are not quite generally true, I do not see that it matters very much.

There is, I believe, not a little significance to be attached to the fact that these often aphoristic remarks are placed in the context of his discussions of the essence of propositions and therefore of language. This discussion extends from *PI* 65 to *PI* 137 and we are frequently reminded (e.g. *PI* 92 and 114) of this background to the discussions of logic and philosophy. This is my justification for considering *PI* 109–133 mainly in connection with that concern about the nature of propositions and language. I shall indeed concentrate on an idea which Wittgenstein says is of 'fundamental importance'. (*PI* 122) This is the idea of a perspicuous representation. It is this idea, I believe, that links the discussions of 'game' and 'proposition' together and, more than any other, provides the clue to the place of these discussions of the nature of philosophy in the context of *PI* 65–137.

One reason why philosophers attach a particular significance to the words 'proposition', 'truth', 'experience' and so on is that they are concerned with general questions about the relation between language and reality. The use of such words in everyday life exhibits so bewildering a variety that it comes to be seen as irrelevant to the philosophical question. At the same time we may pick on one use of the word or one case where the word is used and say that all the others are essentially like this one. Doing this leads to confusion. In such cases we do not command 'a clear view' of how the word is used. What needs to be provided, according to Wittgenstein, is one kind of 'perspicuous representation', something which enables us to see how the various cases where a word is used are related to one another. (*PI* 122) This involves arranging the cases in a certain way so that we can see the connection between very dissimilar cases by seeing a range of cases in between which link them within the same family. As Wittgenstein puts it in the *Philosophical Grammar*:

> What a concept-word indicates is certainly a kinship between objects, but this kinship need not be the sharing of a common property or a constituent. It may connect the objects like the links of a chain, so that one is linked to another *by intermediary links*. Two neighbouring members may have common features and be *similar* to each other, while distant ones belong to the same family without any longer having anything in common. (*Philosophical Grammar*, p. 75)

[1] In his 'Biographical Sketch' in *Ludwig Wittgenstein: A Memoir* (Oxford Paperbacks, 1962), G. H. von Wright remarks: 'Wittgenstein had done no systematic reading in the classics of philosophy. He could read only what he could whole-heartedly assimilate. We have seen that as a young man he read Schopenhauer. From Spinoza, Hume and Kant he said he could get only occasional glimpses of understanding. I do not think that he could have enjoyed Aristotle or Leibniz, two great logicians before him. But it is significant that he did read and enjoy Plato. He must have recognized congenial features, both in Plato's literary and philosophic method and in the temperament behind the thoughts.' (p. 2of.)

In order to show how what we call 'propositions' belong together in one family we need to produce such an arrangement. In order to bring out the connections between apparently diverse cases we need to look for such 'intermediate cases' and even invent them. (*PI* 122) But the purpose of inventing cases is not to reform or refine the rules. (*PI* 132f.) It has the same role as a portrait of an imaginary member of a family might have in an arrangement of portraits designed to bring out the facial characteristics of the family. It is a way of linking two cases which seem to be separate from one another.

It is clear (from *PI* 122, *BB* 125 and elsewhere) that Wittgenstein attached a good deal of importance to the idea of an arrangement of types of case which constituted a 'perspicuous representation' of how they belonged together. The word 'perspicuous' is a translation of the German word 'übersichtlich'. The verb which corresponds to this word is 'übersehen', which in the English translation of *PI* 122 is rendered 'command a clear view'. There is no English word in common use which serves to bring out the connections exactly. Wittgenstein himself seems, in his lectures, to have favoured the word 'synopsis'. But that word has some connotations which are misleading. The word 'surveyable' is in some ways happier than 'perspicuous' and is adopted by the translator of the *Investigations* in *PI* 92 where Wittgenstein writes of the essence of language as 'something that already lies open to view and becomes *surveyable* (*übersichtlich*) by a rearrangement'. Being 'übersichtlich' is a quality expected of a good proof in logic. It is a clarity of presentation which makes it possible to see exactly how each step follows from the one before. Wittgenstein did not, of course, imagine that the different cases of games would be arranged like the steps of a proof. The implication is, however, that a perspicuous or surveyable representation of our use of the word 'game' will enable us to see a series of connections between the range of things we call 'games'. In the allegedly analogous case of 'proposition', the clarity attained by such an arrangement of what we already know would completely dispel the problems surrounding the attempt to state what all propositions have in common.

Notice the emphasis Wittgenstein puts on the uncontroversial character of philosophy. Philosophy is descriptive, leaves everything as it is (*PI* 124), 'puts everything before us' (*PI* 126), 'consists in assembling reminders for a particular purpose'. (*PI* 127) Philosophy tells us nothing we don't know already, does not advance *theses* (*PI* 128) or *explain* anything. (*PI* 126) As he once put it in his 1930–33 Lectures, what he was offering was a 'synopsis of trivialities'.[1] But although the data, so to speak, of philosophy seem individually trivial that does not mean that the work of the philosopher is either easy or unimportant. In *PI* 118 Wittgenstein's 'second voice' raises the question as to where 'our investigation gets its importance from'. To this Wittgenstein replies:

> The results of philosophy are the uncovering of one or another piece of plain nonsense and of bumps that the understanding has got by running its head up against the limits of language. These bumps make us see the value of the discovery. (*PI* 119)

It is worth while to compare Wittgenstein's views as expressed in this and adjacent passages with his view in the *Tractatus*:

> Most of the propositions and questions to be found in philosophical works are not false but nonsensical. Consequently we cannot give any answer to questions

[1] See Moore's *Philosophical Papers*, p. 323.

of this kind, but can only point out that they are nonsensical. Most of the propositions and questions of philosophers arise from our failure to understand the logic of our language.

(They belong to the same class as the question whether the good is more or less identical than the beautiful.) And it is not surprising that the deepest problems are in fact *not* problems at all. (*T* 4.003)

I suggest you now consider what points of similarity and difference strike you between the conception of philosophy in the *Tractatus* and that articulated in the passages of the *Investigations* we have been studying. You may find it helpful, in this connection, to look back at Units 7–10, Sect. VII.3.

Similarities

1 Wittgenstein continued to think that much of what philosophers attempted to ask or say resulted in nonsense and that this in turn was due to misunderstandings of the logic of our language. (See *PI* 92)

2 He sought a method which would put an end to metaphysics. See *T* 6.53. Compare this with *PI* 133. The result of clearing up misunderstandings is that 'the philosophical problems should *completely* disappear'.

3 Philosophical problems are, however, deep. (*T* 4.003, *PI* 111)

Differences

1 The differences mainly arise out of differences in Wittgenstein's conception of logic. The 'logic of our language', according to the *Tractatus*, is something invariant and sublime, whereas in the *Investigations* it is maintained that the philosophy of logic 'speaks of sentences and words in exactly the sense in which we speak of them in ordinary life'. (*PI* 108) The language-games are not directed to 'a future regularization of language' (*PI* 130) but are merely objects of comparison. Whereas, in the *Tractatus*, a model is set up as something 'to which reality *must* correspond' (*PI* 131), the *Investigations* is concerned to acknowledge the diversity of language-games. It does not give a 'once for all' (*PI* 92) answer to questions like '*What is* language?', '*What is* a proposition?'

2 Thus Wittgenstein stresses that while he is concerned to produce 'an order in our knowledge of the use of language' (*PI* 132) he is producing 'one out of many possible orders; not *the* order'. It follows from this that there is no 'final solution' to the problems of philosophy. Whatever Wittgenstein's actual motives for abandoning the study of philosophy after the publication of his *Tractatus*, his doing so was entirely consistent with what he thought he had accomplished. (*T* p. 4) No such claims are made by the author of the *Investigations*. True, he writes that the 'real discovery' is 'the one that makes me capable of stopping philosophy when I want to'. (*PI* 133) But, in the first place, he thought there were serious practical obstacles to attaining the '*complete* clarity' which would make that possible. For part of the philosophical 'disease' is a deep-seated resistance to the cure. He speaks of an 'urge to misunderstand' the workings of language (*PI* 109) whose 'roots are as deep in us as the forms of our language'. (*PI* 111) In the second place, Wittgenstein could no longer regard the work of philosophy as finally done since new forms of language may generate new misunderstandings.

In the *Tractatus*, philosophy is said to be a 'critique of language' (4.0031) which brings out the true 'logical form' of a proposition, as Wittgenstein thought Russell had done in his theory of descriptions with such propositions as 'The author of Waverley was Scotch'. His thought then seemed to be that, once *the* order in our use of language is established, the misunderstandings will be shown for what they are, the nonsenses of philosophy exposed, and so on. In the later philosophy, however, 'many possible orders' in the use of language are admitted. The implication of this seems to be that it would be possible to offer more than one 'perspicuous representation' which would produce the required understanding of our use of words. Instead of there being 'a *single* completely resolved form of every expression' (*PI* 91) there are a number of ways of ordering its use, a number of different arrangements. This is analogous to the ordering of books in a library. There are arrangements which are confusing. Wittgenstein once wrote, in a passage I quoted in the Introduction, that 'some of the greatest achievements in philosophy could only be compared with taking up some books which seemed to belong together, and putting them on a different shelf.' (*BB* 45) We can improve on an arrangement, but there will be nothing final about the new order we have established. Our arrangement is made with a 'particular end in view' (*PI* 132), namely, attaining the kind of clarity which prevents certain misunderstandings. 'A perspicuous representation produces just that understanding which consists in "seeing connections".' (*PI* 122) For this reason it is important to find and indeed *invent* 'intermediate cases'. The licence to *invent* intermediate cases—e.g. think up kinds of game that do not exist in order to bring out how different kinds of game are related—would not exist but for the concern with *an* order rather than *the* order in our use of language. To make use of the analogy of family resemblances, it is like drawing an imaginary member of the family in order to draw attention to resemblances between the faces of different branches of the family that look at first unlike. The invention of language-games may also serve such a purpose. (See *Brown Book*, *BB* 103.)

It is, in some ways, premature to make a study of Wittgenstein's philosophy of philosophy in advance of a wide reading of his work. I have discussed these matters here only because they are embedded by Wittgenstein himself in his discussions of the essence of propositions and of language. Let us consider, then, how they relate to those discussions.

3.4   TOWARDS A 'CLEAR VIEW' OF OUR USE OF 'PROPOSITION' (*PI* 134–137)

Wittgenstein supposed, when he wrote the *Tractatus*, that the essential function of language was to represent how things stand in the world. To know what is essential to something's being a 'proposition' was therefore to know the essence of language. No distinction was drawn between propositions and other types of 'sentence'. The same word indeed is used for both 'proposition' and 'sentence' in the German—the word 'Satz'—and its translation has been a source of difficulty. For example, in *PI* 108, Wittgenstein begins by saying that 'what we call "sentence" and "language" has not the formal unity that I imagined, but is the family of structures more or less related to one another'. The 'formal unity' referred to is the part spoken of in *PI* 65 as the one which caused the 'most headache', namely, 'the part about the *general form of propositions* and of language'. The merit of translating 'Satz' as 'sentence' is that it is very plausible to suppose that language *consists* of sentences. Words, you will remember, are not thought of as having meaning in isolation from their occurrence in sentences. The trouble with translating 'Satz' as 'sentence' is that the 'formal unity' referred to is that of the proposition, that expressed in the idea that propositions are truth-functions of elementary propositions. (*T* 5) There are, as Wittgenstein later came to recognize, confusions here. The English language does not, in this case, encourage them and this poses problems for the translator. 'Why can't you do as you are told?!' is a sentence, evidently enough, but not a proposition, in that sense of 'proposition' in which a proposition is essentially true/false.

How could Wittgenstein have supposed that the formal unity of propositions as presented in the *Tractatus* could also show the essence of language in general? One possible explanation is that he assumed that other kinds of language-use than that involved in making assertions were in some way derivative. There is a footnote to p. 11 of the *Investigations* which may provide some confirmation of this:

> Imagine a picture representing a boxer in a particular stance. Now, this picture can be used to tell someone how he should stand, should hold himself; or how he should not hold himself; or how a particular man did stand in such-and-such a place; and so on.

This passage is concerned with criticism of Frege. And, on this point, Wittgenstein rejected Frege's views when writing the *Tractatus*. Frege had held that every assertion contained an 'assumption' (see *PI* 22) and the picture of the boxer is one Wittgenstein mentions in explanation of that view. But, in the *Tractatus*, Wittgenstein had insisted that propositions do not merely *show* how things stand but also say that they do so stand. (*T* 4.022) So Wittgenstein's 'proposition' cannot be identified with Frege's 'assumption'. Yet it may be that he assumed that orders, questions, and so on had sense, were related to reality, in a derivative but analogous way and that therefore they posed no special problems.

Moore reports Wittgenstein, in 1930, as saying that an *order* expresses a proposition, 'although an order can be neither true nor false, and can be "compared with reality" only in the different sense that you can look to see whether it is carried out or not'.[1] Analogously, we might say, a question is 'compared with reality' by looking to see whether the proposition expressed by a 'Yes' answer is true. This is an alternative way of affirming the primacy of propositions, i.e. of what is true/false, over other kinds of sentence. However Wittgenstein thought this could be done, Russell's remark in the Introduction (*T* p. *x*) that 'The essential business of language is to assert or deny facts' seems to me a fair expression of what he must have believed.

In Wittgenstein's 'transition' period, he had already come to doubt whether propositions and therefore language had the 'formal unity' he had supposed them to have in the *Tractatus*. Moore reports him as saying that the word 'proposition', as generally understood, includes both what he then wanted to call 'propositions' (in a narrow sense suitable to the verification principle), 'hypotheses' and also mathematical propositions. But he then claimed that the 'truth-function' rules apply to all three kinds and that this was why they are all called 'propositions'. By the end of his 1930–33 Lectures, however, he seemed to have moved away from the idea that there is something common to what is called a 'proposition'. Moore writes that he had definitely reached the following conclusion:[2]

> It is more or less arbitrary what we call a 'proposition'... therefore Logic plays a part different from what I and Russell and Frege supposed it to play...

[1] *Philosophical Papers*, p. 262.

[2] *Philosophical Papers*, p. 261.

He went on to say, according to Moore, that 'he could not give a general definition of "proposition" any more than of "game"': that he could only give examples, and that any line he could draw would be 'arbitrary, in the sense that nobody would have decided whether to call so-and-so a "proposition" or not'.

These are themes to which Wittgenstein returns in *PI* 134–137. We cannot say that a proposition is essentially true/false in the sense of the *Tractatus*, namely, that it agrees (or does not agree) with reality. For the general form of propositions, 'This is how things stand' (*T* 4.5), is itself a proposition. And it would be 'obvious nonsense' (*PI* 134) to say that *this* proposition (viz. 'This is how things stand') agrees or fails to agree with reality. It is also, though perhaps less obviously, nonsense to suppose that mathematical propositions agree with reality. If we still want to say that propositions are 'whatever can be true or false' this amounts to saying: 'we call something a proposition when *in our language* we apply the calculus of truth functions to it.' (*PI* 136) We can do various things with what we call a 'proposition'. For example, here is an argument form:

If p, then q:

p

Therefore q.

Anything that can be substituted for the variables 'p' and 'q' is a proposition. The sense in which Wittgenstein accepts that 'true' and 'false' can be said to 'fit' propositions (*PI* 137) is the same sense as that in which we can say that a proposition is what *fits* the places occupied by 'p' and 'q' in such a schema. It is clear that not all sentences will fit into such a schema. Questions and orders do not. There are, Wittgenstein earlier insisted, '*countless* kinds' of sentence. (*PI* 23) This 'multiplicity of kinds of word and sentence' is in striking contrast with 'what logicians have said about the structure of language. (Including the author of the *Tractatus Logico-Philosophicus*.)' The proposition is thus doubly displaced from the kind of central role the *Tractatus* accords to it in an account of meaning and of language. Not only is there no essence of propositions, but, even insofar as we can restrict the word 'proposition' to what is true/false, nothing follows from this about the essence of language. For now a 'proposition' is just one kind of sentence to which Wittgenstein appears not to give any special position. Thus the language-game of *PI* 2, which does not include propositions, is one which we are told could be conceived as 'the whole language of a tribe'. (*PI* 6) If, however, Wittgenstein intended the language-game of *PI* 2 to be so understood, as one in which there are orders but nothing which it true or false, it should be mentioned that this is at variance with his later insistence that if language is to be a 'means of communication' there must be agreement in 'judgments'. (*PI* 242) That insistence seems to mean that propositions, in some sense in which a proposition is whatever is true or false, are indispensable to language.

There are difficulties of interpretation here, to which you will have occasion to return later in the course. But, even if Wittgenstein did continue to accord to propositions a central place in anything that could be called 'language', he did not think that, given an account of propositions, the rest of language would 'take care of itself'. Even if Wittgenstein continued to hold, as has been maintained,[1] that to understand a proposition is to know what is the

[1] For instance, by Roger White. See *Understanding Wittgenstein*, p. 17ff.

57

case if it is true, I do not think he based a general theory of meaning on this. On the contrary, to know the meaning of sentences (e.g. 'I beg your pardon', 'Good morning', and so on) is to know how they can be used in the course of human interchanges: 'the sentence has sense only as a member of a system of language'. (*BB* 42) In any case propositions are just as scattered a family as are games. We can apply the 'calculus of truth-functions' to a whole range of sentences, including:

> 'The class of lions is not a lion'
> 'You ought always to obey your parents'
> '5 times 5 equals 25'
> 'Light travels in straight lines'
> 'Faint heart never won fair maiden'
> 'My watch is lying on the table'

and the *differences* between these are more important than the fact we call them all 'propositions'. I think that Wittgenstein's position here might be expressed by saying that it doesn't much matter what we *call* a proposition, so long as we are clear about those differences. As against the *Tractatus* he himself seemed often to be very liberal in what he was prepared to call a 'proposition'. In his *Remarks on the Foundations of Mathematics*, for example, Wittgenstein wrote:

> What *sort* of proposition is: 'The class of lions is not a lion, but the class of classes is a class'? How is it verified? How could it be *used*?—So far as I can see, only as a grammatical proposition. To draw someone's attention to the fact that the word 'lion' is used in a fundamentally different way from the name of a lion; whereas the class word 'class' is used like the designation of one of the classes, say the class of lions.
>
> ... Even though 'the class of lions is not a lion' seems like nonsense, to which one can only ascribe a sense out of politeness; still I do not want to take it like that, but as a proper sentence [*rechten Satz*], if only it is taken right. (And so not as in the *Tractatus*.) Thus my conception is a different one here. Now this means that I am saying: there is a language-game with this sentence too. (V–29)

But Wittgenstein was inclined to deny that the propositions of logic and mathematics were 'propositions'. He wrote: 'one needs to remember that the propositions of logic are so constructed as to have *no* application as *information* in practice. So it could very well be said that they were not *propositions* at all.' (*Remarks*, Appendix I 20) Again he tended to deny that expressions of sensation were 'statements'. We could call 'I am in pain' a statement, of course, but that might be misleading, 'because "testing", "justification", "confirmation", "refutation" of the statement are connected with the word "statement" in the language-game'. (*Zettel* 549) '2 plus 2 equals 4' and 'I am in pain' stand to the family of propositions perhaps as doodling does to the family of games. Nothing much turns on whether or not we include or exclude them *so long as* we are clear about the differences. There is a tendency to take the propositions of logic or propositions about the immediately given as the most secure members of the class of propositions. That was done by many of the logical positivists. It is that tendency which gives a dialectical point to a denial that they are propositions *at all*.

The place of a perspicuous representation of our use of 'proposition' is to enable us to see how different kinds of proposition are, in spite of their differences, all called 'propositions'. This is something we do by producing examples, according to Wittgenstein, just as in the case of 'games'. (*PI* 135)

Such examples serve to indicate where the problematic boundaries are and thus which are 'borderline' cases of propositions and which are not. In *PI* 134 Wittgenstein includes 'This is how things are' as itself a 'proposition' and takes it as an illustration of 'the fact that *one* feature of our concept of a proposition is, *sounding like a proposition*'. Now Wittgenstein did not wish to say, I am sure, that *anything* which *sounds like* a proposition expressed in English fell under our concept of proposition. He had expressly called this in question in the *Grammar* (p. 113), giving the following as at best 'borderline' cases: 'I am tired', '$2 \times 2 = 4$', 'time passes' and 'there is only one zero'.

Although Wittgenstein thought that propositions did not constitute a sharply defined class, he seems to have wanted to allow that there could be sharply defined *kinds* of proposition. The examples of propositions we give in answer to the question 'What is a proposition?' will include, he writes, 'what one may call inductively defined series of propositions'. (*PI* 135) It is partly in connection with this, I think, that Wittgenstein also invites us to compare the concept of a proposition with the concept of number. When he does this also in the *Grammar* Wittgenstein invites the further comparison with the concept 'cardinal number':

> Compare the concept of proposition with the concept 'number' and then with the concept of cardinal number. We count as numbers cardinal numbers, rational numbers, irrational numbers, complex numbers; whether we call other constructions numbers because of their similarities with these, or draw a definitive boundary here or elsewhere, depends on us. In this respect the concept of number is like the concept of proposition. On the other hand the concept of cardinal number . . . can be called a rigorously circumscribed concept, that's to say it's a concept in a different sense of the word. (p. 113f.)

It is possible to give what is referred to as a 'recursive' definition of 'cardinal number' by means of what Wittgenstein seems to mean by an 'inductively defined series' of numbers. Cardinal numbers, we might say,[1] are those in the following series: 1, 1 + 1, (1 + 1) + 1, ((1 + 1) + 1) + 1, and so on. The class of cardinal numbers is sharply defined, i.e. any given number either belongs to that class or it does not. What is common to all cardinal numbers is this *general form*, i.e. the fact that each is the result of successive applications of the operation +1 to the number 1. What Wittgenstein is conceding here is that *some* kinds of number are like this, but not, as he had supposed in the *Tractatus* (*T* 6.02ff.), *all* numbers. Analogously he allows that our examples of propositions should *include* 'inductively defined series' but denies that all propositions can be obtained as members of such series. Whereas, in the *Tractatus*, he held that 'every proposition is a result of successive applications to elementary propositions' of a particular operation (*T* 6.001), his view in the *Investigations* is that what we call 'proposition' and 'language' does not have 'the formal unity that I imagined, but is the family of structures more or less related to one another'. (*PI* 108) If the analogy between 'proposition' and 'game' is more persuasive, the analogy between 'proposition' and 'number' is more profound.

Wittgenstein does not, in the *Investigations*, provide us with a 'synoptic representation' of our use of 'proposition'. But *PI* 134–137 provides some indication of what such a clear view would accomplish for us. In relation to the *Tractatus* we should see the limitations of that account, not by baldly contradicting it, but by seeing the place of that account in a wider

---

[1] I give this example, which Wittgenstein himself uses in *Remarks on the Foundations of Mathematics*, p. 66., because it needs no further explanation. The omission from the passage of the *Grammar* just quoted is also of an example of recursive definition. But its symbolism is less familiar.

Doesn't baldly contradict account but sees it in a wider perspective [handwritten margin note]

perspective. The clarity which Wittgenstein sought, which would result in the disappearance of philosophical problems (*PI* 133), is likened to the cure of a disease. But, as he put it elsewhere, 'In philosophizing we may not *terminate* a disease of thought. It must run its natural course, and *slow* cure is all important.' (*Zettel* 382) This means, as I understand it, allowing full vent to the ideas which are put forward, including granting assumptions so that they may be developed rather than attempting to suppress the inclination to pursue them. The 'pictures' by which philosophers are captivated lie in language itself. (*PI* 115) We need to be clear as to what it is in language which makes it possible for such 'pictures' to have the hold they have. Once we have done that, they will cease to have such hold.

I believe that this is a fundamental strategy of the early sections of the *Investigations*. One example of this strategy is in the method of *PI* 2, in which Wittgenstein considers a language-game 'for which the description given by Augustine is right'. This method is applied also to the passage of Plato quoted in *PI* 46 and is quite expressly put forward by Wittgenstein as an application of the *same* method. (*PI* 48) He later writes: 'There is not *a* philosophical method, though there are indeed methods, like different therapies'. (*PI* 133) A major concern of the earlier sections had been to get a clear view of the relation between our use of 'name' and of 'meaning'. This was accomplished by studying 'the phenomena of language in primitive kinds of application'. (*PI* 5)

The strategy of *PI* 134–137 is the same but the method is different. Wittgenstein argues, as we have seen, that the *Tractatus* account of the essence of propositions is not only inadequate as an account of the essence of language but cannot be right as an account of propositions. A clear view of our use of 'proposition' would indeed allow that some propositions belong to the class of 'propositions' because they can be generated out of other propositions. But, at bottom, the *Tractatus* account of propositions involves what Wittgenstein came to regard as a 'bad picture' of the relation between something's being a 'proposition' and its being 'true or false'. Part of what is wrong with it lies in the account of elementary propositions which requires that to be 'true or false' is to be a 'picture' of reality. That view, insofar as it is expressed in the claim that 'elementary propositions . . . consist of names in immediate combination' (*T* 4.221), has already been shown to embody a false conception of the relation between naming and meaning. We are left, then, with the bare contention that, as Wittgenstein put it in the *Notebooks* of 1914–18: 'Every proposition is essentially true-false'. Put like that, it sounds as if being true or false were some independent characteristic that all and only propositions have, as though it could be used to determine what is and what is not a proposition. Whereas, as Wittgenstein points out in *PI* 136, it is simply that we only use the word 'proposition' of sentences after which we could appropriately put '. . . is true' or '. . . is false'. A child might be taught the use of the word 'proposition' by being told 'Ask yourself if you can say "is true" after it. If these words fit, it's a proposition.' (*PI* 137) But he is not thereby told what the essence of propositions is.

On the contrary, none of the problems about deciding borderline cases of propositions turn on the question whether we can say 'is true' or 'is false' after such cases. Our reluctance to say '$2 \times 2 = 4$' is *true* is just another manifestation of our reluctance to regard it as a *proposition*. So too is our willingness to regard it as *true*, if we do not share Wittgenstein's reservations on this point. I do not think it was, for Wittgenstein, important which way we decided such borderline cases. It was, nonetheless, important to recognize that they were, at best, peripheral cases. If we do not recognize this, then we shall be tempted to construe mathematical propositions on the model of empirical propositions and suppose there must be some mathematical reality to which true mathematical propositions correspond. There are, Wittgenstein came to think, other meaningful sentential forms than the kind labelled 'propositions', sentences therefore whose meaning could not be identified with truth-conditions since neither 'is true' nor 'is false' could be added after them. Our understanding of arithmetical propositions, Wittgenstein thought, is shown by the use we make of them. We follow certain rules when we multiply, check our counting, and so on. And these rules can be stated. But, Wittgenstein asks: 'Might we not do arithmetic without having the idea of uttering arithmetical *propositions*, and without ever having been struck by the similarity between a multiplication and a proposition?'[1] This is a question to which Wittgenstein was inclined to answer, 'Yes'.

An account of propositions thus ceases to have the central place accorded to it in the *Tractatus*. There seems to be a separation, in the *Investigations*, of an account of the meaning of a sentence from questions about truth-conditions. That there is such a separation is a matter of controversy which is taken up by Samuel Guttenplan in Unit 32.

---

[1] *Remarks on the Foundations of Mathematics*, p. 49. This is from one of the sections which, according to Wittgenstein's literary executors, Wittgenstein must have intended to include in the *Philosophical Investigations*.

QUESTIONS FOR DISCUSSION AND REVISION

1 What is a 'language-game'? What use does Wittgenstein make of language-games in the early sections of the *Philosophical Investigations*?

2 What role, if any, does pointing to an object play in teaching language?

3 To what extent, if at all, does Wittgenstein's discussion of 'simples' in the *Investigations* undermine the doctrines of the *Tractatus*?

4 What points of resemblance and difference, between Wittgenstein's earlier and his later views on the nature of logic, strike you as most significant? Which view, if either, do you think is right?

5 What purpose is served by Wittgenstein's comparison of the concept 'proposition' with the concept 'game'?

Destroys — The ultimate constituents of propositions are names & that the world is a configuration of objects named by those names.

names — rejects ostensive definition substituting language games.

Simple objects — rejects absolute simplicity — in favour of what is relative to some particular use or context.

Not explicitly contradicted

(i) Propositions are pictures

(ii) Truth functions of elementary propositions

— Picture theory seems to assume that propositions serve one & only one essential purpose — if a thing is true or false.

FURTHER READING

Attention has been focused, in these units, on part of the *Philosophical Investigations*. There are other texts of Wittgenstein, however, which are highly relevant to the themes we have been discussing:

> *Philosophical Grammar*, ed. Rush Rhees, trans. Anthony Kenny, Oxford, Blackwell, 1974, esp. Part I, Sects. III, IV, VI, IX and Appendix 3.
>
> *The Brown Book*, a preliminary study for the '*Philosophical Investigations*', whose early sections have some points of striking resemblance with the sections we have been studying.
>
> *The Blue Book*, esp. *BB.* 1–46.
>
> *Remarks on the Foundations of Mathematics*, tr. G. E. M. Anscombe, Blackwell, 1956. It seems that Wittgenstein at one time intended to include a large section on the philosophy of mathematics in the *Investigations*, as he had done in the *Grammar*. Part I of these *Remarks* is part of an earlier draft manuscript of the *Investigations*.

Wittgenstein's lectures in 1930–33 also contain relevant discussions. Moore's notes on them originally appeared as 'Wittgenstein's Lectures in 1930–33' in *Mind, Vol.* LXIII, 1954, and *Vol.* LXIV, 1955. They are reprinted in a collection of Moore's own papers, *Philosophical Papers*, Allen and Unwin, 1959, Ch. XI.

There is a very extensive literature about Wittgenstein's later philosophy, much of it detailed by K. T. Fann in the bibliography appended to his *Wittgenstein's Conception of Philosophy*, Blackwell, 1969. The following is a limited list of papers relevant to the topics discussed in these units:

> Cavell (Stanley): 'The availability of Wittgenstein's later philosophy', *The Philosophical Review*, 1962, included in G. Pitcher (ed.) *Wittgenstein: The Philosophical Investigations*, Macmillan Papermac, 1968, pp. 151ff.
>
> Feyerabend (Paul): 'Wittgenstein's *Philosophical Investigations*', *Philosophical Review*, 1955; also included in the Pitcher collection, pp. 104ff.
>
> Rhees (Rush): 'Wittgenstein's Builders', *Proceedings of the Aristotelian Society*, 1959–60, reprinted in a collection of papers by Rhees, *Discussions of Wittgenstein*, Routledge and Kegan Paul, 1970.
>
> White (Roger): 'Can whether one proposition makes sense depend on the truth of another? (*Tractatus* 2.0211–2)', in *Understanding Wittgenstein*, Royal Institute of Philosophy Lectures, Vol. 7, 1972/73, ed. Godfrey Vesey, Macmillan, 1974, pp. 14ff.

THOUGHT AND REALITY: CENTRAL THEMES IN WITTGENSTEIN'S PHILOSOPHY

1–2   CARTESIAN SCEPTICISM

3–4   JOHN LOCKE: THE FOUNDATIONS OF EMPIRICISM

5–6   REALISM AND LOGICAL ANALYSIS

7–10   SAYING AND SHOWING: AN INTRODUCTION TO
        WITTGENSTEIN'S 'TRACTATUS LOGICO-PHILOSOPHICUS'

11–13   VERIFICATION AND MEANING

14–15   LANGUAGE AND REALITY: 'PHILOSOPHICAL
        INVESTIGATIONS' 1–137

16–19   MEANING AND UNDERSTANDING: LOCKE AND
        WITTGENSTEIN

20–22   LANGUAGE AND THE PRIVACY OF EXPERIENCE

23–24   THE GRAMMAR OF FEELINGS

25–26   SOLIPSISM AND THE SELF

27–28   THE WILL

29–31   CERTAINTY

32   MEANING AND TRUTH

[Handwritten notes:]

— Truth function rule applies

(i) Propositions are either True or false
    " " derivatives of elementary propositions
(ii)
(iii) Propositions show how things stand

P. 1 Moves away from idea that there
is something in common to what is called
a proposition — ie games cannot
give definition — he did not
Think that given an account of ~~default~~
Proposition the rest would take care of itself